MW00983939

POLARIZED
Sex, Lies, and Family Betrayal

POLARIZED

Sex, Lies, and Family Betrayal

A MEMOIR
OF MANIC DEPRESSION

JOSEPH DEBLASI

DAR PRESS

Polarized: Sex, Lies, and Family Betrayal
A Memoir of Manic Depression
Copyright © 2014 Joseph DeBlasi
Published by Dar Press

All rights reserved. No part of this book may be reproduced (except for inclusion in reviews), disseminated or utilized in any form or by any means, electronic or mechanical, including photocopying, recording, or in any information storage and retrieval system, or the Internet/World Wide Web without written permission from the author or publisher.

For more information email the author: Joefd@icloud.com

Printed in the United States of America

Polarized: Sex, Lies, and Family Betrayal
A Memoir of Manic Depression
Joseph DeBlasi

1. Title   2. Author   3. Memoir

Library of Congress Control Number: 2013951681

ISBN 13: 978-0-615-89565-9

Dedicated to Grandma Dar.
For one hundred years you have demonstrated
that life is indeed what you make of it.

TABLE OF CONTENTS

PROLOGUE

FEBRUARY 2000

The noontime glare hit me full in the face, turning my eyes to angry slits. The sun is strong in Florida even in February and even worse when you're flat on your back with no means to shield your eyes. Still the warmth felt nice; it made me think of playing baseball. A shadow fell across my face, and I opened them slightly to see a thirtyish-year-old man staring down at me with a puzzled, slightly stupid expression. That was when I realized I had spoken out loud.

"I'm gonna play for the Mets," I repeated.

"Sure, buddy," he monotoned.

"You don't know who I am."

A second guy, standing down by my feet, studied me for a

second, and I knew from his smirk that he *did* recognize me. "Sure we do," he said as much to his friend as to me. "We know exactly who you are."

"We do?" The first guy looked down at me again, this time with a dubious expression.

Damn straight you do. Just the other day, I'd made every sports page in New York and even a few of the radio shows for my performance on the field.

"Yeah, this is the clown who showed up at the Mets training facility thinking he was gonna get a tryout."

"No shit." Now the first guy's expression was a mix of humor and pity, kind of like I was a zoo animal and he'd just found out I could do tricks. He was probably wondering why he'd chosen a vocation that involved dealing with criminals and crazies.

Either way he was a wiseass, but luckily for him I couldn't do much about it. These guys weren't a couple of curious onlookers but heavily muscled corrections officers who, for all their "aw shucks" demeanor, could put me down in about two seconds. And I wasn't lying on a beach taking in the rays after winning a game; I was strapped to a gurney so I couldn't cause any problems while being transported from Sharpes correctional facility to the Circles of Care psychiatric hospital.

I hadn't bothered to struggle when they bound my arms and legs; I had been shackled before and knew there was no use in trying to get free. After all this wasn't my first trip to the ball game. *Ball game.* I laughed at the irony because it was my trip to the ball game that had begun my latest spiral into the bell jar. The officers were staring at me again, this time with annoyance. *Screw 'em if they can't take a joke*, I thought and closed my eyes again. I was just glad to be getting out of this dump. Surely the treatment would be better once I got to Circles. The people down here might be bunch of hicks, but the doctors at a psychiatric hospital had to have heard of manic depression.

The EMTs loaded me none too gently into the ambulance, then, with two quick pounds of a fist against the side, signaled the driver to move it out. A second later we pulled onto the street, sirens blaring. I guess I should have been concerned about going to a new hospital, but I wasn't. By my calculations it wouldn't take more than a day or two to convince the shrinks it was perfectly safe to release me back into society. After all I had fooled some of the best doctors back in New York—had been fooling them for years—and couldn't imagine this time would be any different.

I was looking forward to it, actually. I always got a high—admittedly a relative term in my present condition—when I talked my way out of a facility. It was a giddy "and the Oscar goes to..." type of sensation. But the *real* fun was when I inevitably returned a few days later, after committing some even stranger act, and saw the looks on the faces of the staff. They were always shocked that despite their extensive medical training, I'd been able to sell them a bill of goods. With that cheerful thought, I melted into the gurney and stared up at the ceiling of the ambulance, already planning my spiel for the staff who would be unfortunate enough to be working when I arrived.

When deciding whether to commit someone to a locked mental ward, a medical team looks primarily at two factors: namely whether the person poses a danger to him or herself and whether he or she poses a danger to others. In my case—and, I suspect, in the cases of many other people suffering from bipolar disorder—the answer to both of these questions is it depends on the present circumstances and where I am in the cycle of the disease. For example when I am manic, there are certain go-to obsessions that consume my every waking moment. This could be a monetary object I have to acquire, a person I have to see, or an inappropriate activity I have to undertake. If someone gets in the way of my getting what I want, I am quite capable of hurting them. When I am in the depression phase, however, I barely have the energy to get out of bed. During these times I am capable of hurting only myself. And when I am "normal"—a relative term that means I'm stable on my meds—I am capable of hurting no one. The thing is, unlike a jail sentence, there is no end date to incarceration in a mental hospital; you are not suddenly released the moment you feel better. The other issue is that decisions regarding your freedom are based on a particular doctor's subjective assessment.

So, as confident as I was in my ability to con the medical community, there was still always the chance that some doctor might not buy my story. This upped the stakes; however, it also made it that much more pleasurable when, after witnessing my performance, the doctor signed the release papers. I was still mentally rehearsing my lines when the ambulance rolled to a stop and two Circles staffers made sure I was still securely shackled before unloading my gurney from the back.

Keeping in mind that "less is more" in such a situation, I would explain in the simplest terms that there was a very rational explanation for my behavior. I wouldn't even mention the thing with the Mets because it had nothing to do with my present predicament, at least not directly.

A few nights after that fiasco, I asked my mother to fly with me to New York to see my father, Dr. Joseph DeBlasi. She refused, which was unacceptable to me. I hadn't intended to scare her and *never* would have thrown her over the balcony of her fifth-floor beachfront condo as I threatened. I just needed her to understand why it was imperative that I see my father, whom I hadn't spoken to in years, and why we had to leave *that minute*. Truly the only reason I rolled her up in the mattress was to make her listen to me, and she would have if only my stepfather hadn't called the cops.

The next thing I knew, I was arrested, taken from the house in cuffs, and later formally charged with assault and battery. Bail was set at fifteen thousand dollars—Florida's version of tough love, apparently. This would be an important point to make with Circle's staff, that it was a grave injustice to throw someone with manic depression in jail like a common criminal. I ran through the script, noting with satisfaction that it sounded perfectly logical; still a small part of me realized that whomever I spoke with might feel differently.

It also hadn't escaped me that I would be performing without my usual audience. My brothers, Kevin and Stephen, were both out of the country. Kevin was vacationing in Argentina with his then-fiancée and her parents, and Stephen and his wife were in Paris on business. Jacqueline, my on-again, off-again girlfriend of four years, wouldn't be there either. In those days we were mostly off and had been since our last trip to Puerto Rico. She had refused the several phone calls I had placed from jail. Besides, there was no way she could post bail. She was still paying off the gambling debts and phone bills I had run up on her credit card at the Hotel San Juan.

Had Kevin (who, in addition to being an attorney, is my biggest advocate) been there, the incident with my mother wouldn't have happened at all; in all likelihood my stunt with the Mets wouldn't have gone as far as it did. After all he had stepped in the last time I'd decided it was time to fulfill my lifelong dream of becoming a professional athlete. In the autumn of 1998, I had waged a two-month campaign of terror to get myself a tryout for the New York Jets. When my initial overtures were ignored, I moved on to more aggressive tactics such as screaming, "You'll find bodies in dumpsters if I don't get this tryout!"

That was when the ever-resourceful Kevin stepped in. After finagling a meeting with the Jets' head of security, he used his considerable skills of persuasion to convince the guy it would be prudent—and safer— simply to give me a tryout. Manic depressives, he explained, can be extremely determined, and I was unlikely to go away quietly. Amazingly enough the security head agreed; even more incredible was that he was able to convince Jets Coach Bill Parcells to give me a shot.

But the real kicker was where the tryouts were held: Hofstra University in Hempstead, Long Island. I was well acquainted with the place, having been a student there until I was banned from campus for "bizarre and menacing" behavior. For most of 1998, I was Hofstra security's public enemy number one—my photo was even prominently displayed in all of their security offices. But in October of that year, the powers that be had inexplicably allowed me to return to their MBA program. Now the same security officers who had barred me from the grounds looked on in shock as I ran through a full official Jets tryout. I didn't make the cut, of course, but it didn't matter. The Jets had held up their end of the bargain, so after they showed me and Kevin the door, I never bothered them again.

Baseball was another story, though. I knew the Mets training camp was in Port St. Lucie, only an hour's drive from my mom's condo. So when mania struck that sunny morning, I grabbed my bat and glove and jumped in the car. The fact that I didn't have an invitation to try out didn't deter me; neither did the fact that I hadn't even been good enough to make the Rutgers team fourteen years earlier. I was living in the manic zone of all possibilities, and if I'd had my heart set on being an astronaut I would have thought nothing of driving to Cape Canaveral and strong-arming my way into NASA.

I walked into the Port St. Lucie training facility glove in hand, ready to show the Mets officials what an asset I'd be to the team. They weren't interested, however, and after a few choice words on my part, they threw me out with a warning not to return. To me this was nothing more than a challenge. If they could not see what I was capable of, well, I would just have to convince them otherwise.

That was my intent when I returned the following day. And when they didn't listen to reason—namely my claims that Bill Parcells had personally set up the tryout for me and that I had a better arm than Mike Piazza—I became more forceful. In the end it really didn't amount to much more than a few curses and threats, so I was rather surprised when the cops showed up and placed me under arrest. I was charged with trespassing after a warning, a misdemeanor. This led me to believe that had I done to the Mets half of what I had done to the Jets, the Port St. Lucie police would have put me in front of a firing squad.

Had Kevin been with me in Florida, he undoubtedly would have explained the situation to the Mets; he certainly would have made sure the story was kept out of the papers. As it was, however, my little escapade was covered by the Associated Press. And, as luck would have it, February 25 was a slow day in the world of sports, so my run-in with the Mets was the big scoop. All four major New York papers picked up the story, and every New York sports radio broadcaster was jabbering on about the nut who was trying to get onto the Mets. I was named "jerk of the week" in a prominent sports magazine, and ESPN's Peter Gammons quipped that it was not such a stretch that I had a better throwing arm than Mike Piazza. One smartass wrote that I "apparently couldn't wait for this year's Mets fantasy camp" while another opined that my only tryout was going to be for the prison team. One of the papers described the day's events as if they were an episode of *The Sopranos*, allegedly because in addition to the $2,000 in my pocket, I carried an attitude, used vulgar language, and was an Italian from New York.

The coverage of the story, while fairly predictable (and, when seen from the perspective of someone who has never had to deal with manic depression, even a bit humorous), was also indicative of how those suffering from this disease are depicted by the media. Our stories are written to portray the same polarities from which we suffer. We are either the scary, threatening figures who commit heinous acts or comical whack jobs. How many people laughed while reading my story on the subway on the way to work? Nearly as many, I suppose, as the number who would have cried had my adventure—or, God forbid, the incident with my mother—taken an uglier turn. Either way they never quite got the entire story.

If, for example, any of these writers had followed me for a few more hours, they would have learned that I had bonded myself out of the Mets' trespassing charge with the disability I was collecting from my former employer, the American International Group (AIG). And had they dug a little deeper, they might have learned that when in the grips of mania I not only harass members of sports franchises, but I'm also capable of menacing my own family.

If they had stuck with me the rest of that week, they would have learned that I was indeed able to dupe the psychiatrists at Circles of Care. However, the only person I outsmarted was myself, for after I convinced them of my sanity I was not released as I had assumed I'd be but sent back to Sharpes correctional facility, where I would spend the next month among murderers, rapists, and other dregs of society. So much for my misguided belief that manic depression operates as a get-out-of-jail-free card.

In other words had any of these reporters bothered to look past the punch line, they would have found the much darker story of a life torn in two. They would have found a person who is so manic one week he believes he can play for the Mets and so depressed the next all he can think about is killing himself. But even more than that, they would have found a life torn between two families, two homes, and two identities. That day at the Mets camp, they saw a man desperate enough to do anything; if they had looked a little harder they would have found the high school boy so timid he asked his father to call the baseball coach to find out how he could get on the team.

Finally, if they had done a little research on my life as well as my disease, they would have discovered that while I may be genetically predisposed to manic depression, it probably would not have manifested—at least not to such a severe degree—but for the traumatic events of my childhood. But none of these writers bothered to do that; instead they focused on the moment "that nut" materialized at the Mets' training facility.

That is why I am writing this story: not just for myself but for everyone suffering with this disease. Most importantly I am writing it in the hope that the next time a nut makes the news, people will look for the real story behind the sound bite.

CHAPTER 1

That's Amore

If in 2000 my story sounded like something from *One Flew Over the Cuckoo's Nest*, it began more like *Moonstruck* in the Canarsie section of Brooklyn. While these days Canarsie is known for white flight and decline, back in the 1950s and '60s the neighborhood was a bustling mix of Germans, Jews, and Italians who had survived the Depression and World War II and were ready for a taste of the American dream. Both sides of my family—the Sicilian DeBlasis and the Neapolitan Paladinos—were among them. It was under this umbrella of optimism, hope, and ambition that my parents, Joseph DeBlasi and Regina Paladino, grew up.

Although the DeBlasis and Paladinos knew of each other from around the neighborhood, my parents didn't officially meet until they were sixteen. One morning on the way to their respective Catholic high schools, they caught sight of each other across a crowded subway car. Soon after that they went on their first date. Smitten with the petite, attractive Regina, Joseph didn't wait long before asking her to go steady with him. When she wanted to take it slow and date other boys, he pursued her relentlessly, bringing flowers to both her and her mother every time he picked her up for a date. To this day my maternal grandmother—Grandma Dar, as my brothers and I call her—swears that Joseph DeBlasi was one of the nicest and most respectful boys in Canarsie, which was probably why she was so stunned by the way things turned out. But that was years in the future; for now it seemed like a romance made in heaven—or at least in Brooklyn.

Although both my mother and father were from working-class Italian families, that was where the similarities ended. The Paladinos were a loving, low-key bunch who enjoyed a simple life centered around family and hard work "My childhood was so normal, it could have been a 1950s sitcom," my mother likes to say; this she attributes largely to her parents' loving marriage. Her father, Giacomo "Jack" Paladino, was a mild-mannered cabinetmaker known for his dry sense of humor and the foresight to leave Naples in the mid-1930s, before Fascism and war decimated Europe. As was common for Italians in those days, he headed for Buenos Aires but eventually came to the conclusion that his job prospects were better in the United States. His brother, Vincent, was already living in Canarsie and making a decent living in the construction business, so in 1941 Jack joined him. Jack was happy to be reunited with his brother, but he was even happier when he met Vincent's wife's cousin, Chiara "Clara" Zullo.

One warm summer day, Jack was in Astoria, Queens, doing some work on the second floor of the Zullos' apartment house. As he stood up to stretch his legs and gulp down some ice water, he noticed a beautiful girl reading a book in the backyard. While Clara was taking in the sun, he was taking in her great legs. At thirty-seven Jack was strikingly handsome with ice-blue eyes, wavy dark hair, and a smile that stopped women in their tracks. My brothers and I joke that Grandpa Jack must have gotten crabs in at least nine different South American countries, but once he saw my grandmother his days as a Casanova were over. They were married by a justice of the peace in 1942, just in time to save Jack from being deported.

By that time the US was fully entrenched in World War II, and the State Department was on the hunt for any German, Japanese, or Italian spies operating on American soil. One of the Italians they were tracking happened to be named Giacomo Paladino, and it didn't take them long to come after Jack. He spent the next four months interned at Ellis Island with only letters from his young wife to keep him going. Finally the Feds figured out they had interned the wrong man, and they let him go. In June 1942 Jack and Grandma Dar were officially married by the Catholic Church, and she was sure to let us know that "nothing went on in the bedroom until we were wed in the eyes of God."

Clara and Jack wasted no time in starting a family. My mother, Regina, was born on March 22, 1943, and three and a half years later her sister Paula followed. The four of them lived in an apartment house in Canarsie, and Jack continued building houses for his older brother, Vincent. Like most young families, they struggled financially, but there was never a shortage of love. The apartment didn't have much heat, and on chilly nights Grandpa Jack used to lay his wool overcoat over his sleeping daughters. He may not have known Mom was awake, but to this day it's one of her most precious childhood memories.

Thanks to Clara's skill as a seamstress, there was never a shortage of beautiful clothes. She lovingly sewed every shirt, skirt, and dress so my mother and Aunt Paula didn't have to wear hand-me-downs like so many of their classmates. By 1956 my grandparents had saved enough money to move into their own home, a brick two-family built by my grandfather and his brother. It was in this house on East Ninety-First Street and Flatlands Avenue that my brothers and I would spend many happy times; in fact it helped provide stability during the roughest years of our childhood.

There were of course the usual family quarrels. Grandpa Jack was very overprotective of his daughters when it came to boys (although probably no more than any other Italian father), and Grandma Dar—well, let's just say that today she'd be investigated by child protective services. Even if they overlooked the time she threw a freshly skinned chicken at my mother as she walked in the door late for dinner, they definitely would have had a problem with the time she locked her daughters out of the apartment—without their shoes—as punishment for misbehaving. But overall my mother's child-hood was very happy and one my mother hoped to emulate one day with her own family. Grandma Dar sometimes got angry with my grandfather over his meddling sisters, but as my mother always said, "If that's all Grandma had to complain about in her marriage, she did pretty well."

The DeBlasis—my father's side of the family—were also loving and close-knit, but, like most Sicilians, they were showier and a bit more boisterous. They appeared to have more money than the Paladinos as well a certain air of mystery surrounding them. My paternal grandfather, Francis "Frank" DeBlasi, was born in Brooklyn in 1913. He was tall and slender with movie-star looks and a thin, black Clark Gable mustache. His parents had emigrated from Sicily at the beginning of the century and owned a bakery in Canarsie. As a teenager Grandpa Frank delivered bread for the bakery and drove a milk truck. Later he worked for a few years in the garment district, but no one really knows what he did after that for the simple fact that he would never give anyone a straight answer.

This may be why the Paladinos always speculated that Grandpa Frank was involved in some shady criminal enter-prise, especially after they heard rumors that he had spent some time in jail. We knew he had some "associates" in the garment industry, but if anyone was going to be "made" it would have been his wife, our Grandma Jennie. She was the toughest, hardest-working, most opinionated woman you would ever want to meet. She wore not only the pants in their relationship but the shoes, the socks, and the jockstrap as well.

There were some secrets buried in Grandma Jennie's family, the Terminis. Born Vincenzina Termini in 1920, my grandmother later unofficially changed her name to the Anglicized "Jennie" to avoid being teased by the other kids at school. Her father, Michael Termini, was a thin, wiry man with skin so dark he could have passed for black. Michael had married Jennie's mother, Patricia, after his first wife was killed in a *mysterious* car accident. He and Patricia raised his three children from that marriage and added two of their own—Jennie and her brother Mike.

Patricia had a conspicuous linear scar on her otherwise beautiful face, but no one ever spoke about how Great-Grandma Termini had gotten the wound. Couple that with Grandma Jennie's silence about her father's first marriage, and people began to speculate that he had been involved in a tragic love triangle. Whatever the case he was by all accounts a good husband and father, and, as a foreman in Jersey, a good provider. The family lived in a large two-story house in Canarsie, and as my grandma Jennie always said, "We never went without, even during the Depression."

Jennie was smart as a whip, making straight A's in school and graduating with honors, but it was her extraordinary skills in the kitchen that made her famous in the neighborhood. Under the careful tutelage of her mother, she was soon making cannoli good enough to bring grown men to tears. But that wasn't what caught the attention of Frank DeBlasi, who lived around the corner from the Terminis and was friends with Jennie's brother. With her beautiful strawberry-blond hair and shapely figure, Jennie was quite a looker. The problem was that although she looked like a grown woman, she was only thirteen. Frank was already a man of twenty, and, needless to say, this did not go over well with the men in Jennie's family. Thankfully cooler heads prevailed, and everyone agreed that Frank and Jennie wouldn't court until she turned sixteen. They were married on October 30, 1938, the same night Orson Well's *War of the Worlds* terrified thousands of gullible Americans.

My father, Joseph DeBlasi, came into the world on December 31, 1942, after twenty- four hours of labor and, finally, an emergency Caesarian section. Giving birth to an eleven- pound baby nearly killed Grandma Jennie; she lost several liters of blood and remained hospitalized for weeks. But any suffering was a faint memory as soon as she laid eyes on "her Joseph," especially his beautiful red hair. Even after he stopped speaking to her many years later, her eyes still lit up whenever she spoke of those bright-red locks. One of her favorite things to do was wash them. In fact I think she washed his hair for him until he started losing it at age twenty-two, the same year he married my mother.

While red hair is considered a bit unusual for Italians, it wasn't a shock for little Joe. After all both his mother and grandmother Termini had strawberry-blond hair. No matter that her Joseph's was more orange than strawberry and a bit reminiscent of Bozo; she loved it anyway.

After Jennie recovered she and Frank returned to the Termini home to live with her parents and brother. The birth had been so difficult that Jennie would wait nearly eight years to have another child. My father spent his early years surrounded by five fawning adults—the word *spoiled* doesn't come close to describing it. He slept in his crib until he was six, and the high chair was his throne until the age of seven. He was the king of the house and, as far as Jennie was concerned, the world. When my uncle Mike was born in 1950, he didn't have a prayer; he wasn't the daughter Jennie had longed for, and he didn't have his brother's beautiful red hair.

From the time her Joseph was old enough to crawl, Jennie told everyone how he was going to be a doctor, which, for Italians, was even better than having a child become a priest. Still Jennie covered all bases by signing him up to be an altar boy at Our Lady of Miracles Church and by bringing her famous creampuffs to the bishop whenever he was in town. Life was good, and under the careful cultivation of Grandma Jennie, my father grew up strong and certain of his place in the world. One might say he believed himself to be the *center* of the world, but that would come later. Back then he was just a skinny, red-haired kid who had reached his full height of six feet, four inches by the time he was a teenager.

Jennie was fiercely protective of her Joseph even compared to other Italian mamas. When a boy fitting his description was spotted walking away from PS 114 after breaking a window, one of the parents called the principal to finger my father. And who could blame her? There were not too many redheaded giants trolling the streets of Canarsie.

Grandma Jennie wasn't interested in the odds, however. As soon as she heard her Joseph had been accused, she went right to the school, barged into the principal's office, and yelled dramatically, "It was not my Joseph who did such a thing! He was home studying at the time."

The kicker was she was right. A tall redheaded kid visiting from out of town was the culprit. While most people would have settled for a simple apology, Grandma Jennie insisted that the accuser go to the school and apologize to both her and her Joseph over the loudspeaker! And he did it, too, right after the Pledge of Allegiance.

Given her attachment to her Joseph, it was no surprise that Grandma Jennie wasn't exactly thrilled to hear he was dating Regina Paladino. It wasn't that she had a problem with my mother—or, at least, no more of a problem than she would have had with any girl. But her Joseph was only sixteen years old, and she wasn't ready to share him yet. Besides he was going to be a doctor, and a girlfriend was bound to interfere with his studies.

I can picture my grandmother employing a combination of guilt, concern, and talking hands as she stated her case. But her protests fell on deaf ears. Joseph was crazy about Regina, and there was nothing his mother could do about it. One night he strolled over to the Paladinos' for a visit only to be told by my grandma Dar that she had gone to the movies with Frankie Piero, another kid from the neighborhood. When Joseph heard the news, he began to cry and, according to my grandma Dar, was inconsolable.

Mom must have been a sucker for a sensitive guy, because after that night, she caved. From that moment on she and

Joseph were inseparable; they went steady for the rest of high school and all through college. Eventually even Grandma Jennie resigned herself to the fact that they were going to get married. Although no one would ever be good enough for her Joseph, he could have done worse. Mom was attractive and respectful, and Grandma Jennie's own mother adored her. Mom also came from a respected Italian family. All right, the Paladinos weren't Sicilian, but at least they weren't Jews, which at that time would have been considered an *infamnia*.

What pleased Grandma Jennie most was that mom was onboard with Joseph's plan to become a doctor. While the professional hopes for the family rested on him, my mother was actually a much better student; in fact she often wrote his papers so he could keep up with the other kids at Brooklyn College. After his graduation they got engaged, and Mom got her first teaching job at Abraham Lincoln Junior High. She saved every penny she earned so they'd have enough to sustain them while Joseph was in medical school. This was music to Grandma Jennie's ears. Her Joseph was marrying not only a private tutor but a cash cow!

To help out with expenses, Grandma Jennie also took her first job, as a bookkeeper for the Abraham & Strauss department store. After quickly making a name for herself as a diligent and efficient worker, she took a position with the Internal Revenue Service, where she also rose rapidly up the ranks. (Ironically the IRS sent Grandma Jennie to take classes at Hofstra University, the same campus I would be banned from years later for my scary manic behavior.) Every extra cent that came into the DeBlasi house was earmarked for her Joseph's tuition. My Uncle Mike, who was in high school at the time, couldn't even get a limo for his prom. "Joseph will buy you a limo when he becomes a rich doctor," my grandmother assured him. "He is going to take care of all of us."

While neither money nor my mother was standing in the way of Joseph's medical degree, his grades were. While at Brooklyn College he had pulled "gentlemen's hooks"—C grades—in several classes including calculus. With a GPA like that, he wasn't getting into mortuary school let alone medical school. Fortunately for him it is not what you know but who you know. Grandpa Frank had some friends with influence over a Jewish politician, and the politician knew people at Chicago Medical School. As part of the deal, my father would first have to do a one-year unpaid fellowship there, but that didn't matter as long as he ended up an MD. My grandmother continued to work her fingers to the bone, and my mother agreed to spend the next five years away from her friends and family. They married in Brooklyn on July 11, 1965, then headed to Chicago.

The first few years of their marriage were busy but happy. Like most upwardly mobile couples, my parents were short on both money and time while they worked toward their goals. Each month they struggled to pay the bills—or at least my mother did. While Joseph attended medical school full-time, Mom supported them by teaching biology to inner-city high school kids. At night she took graduate classes at Northwestern University, and in June 1968 she received her master's in biology. She wanted to go to the graduation ceremony but missed it because my father was anxious to get home to Grandma Jennie over the summer break.

In 1968 Chicago, like many of the big cities around the nation, was rocked by race riots. On the day I was born, November 9, 1968, it rocked a little more. An earthquake literally struck the city. It was only a minor one, but to a city that hadn't felt a quake in years, it was quite an event.

Like the earthquake I was unplanned. At eight pounds, six ounces, I didn't weigh nearly as much as my father had, but I did get his name. My mother broke with the Italian tradition of naming the firstborn son after the paternal grandfather for no other reason than she didn't like the name Francis. Grandpa Frank wasn't thrilled by this, so they threw him a bone by using Francis for my middle name. Grandma Jennie got over the perceived insult by embracing the idea of having a Joe Jr. in the family.

I might not have had my father's red hair, but my parents adored me just the same. Even though they didn't have a lot of money, I wanted for nothing. For my first birthday I received a little red car I could sit in. By my second birthday, I was driving around our apartment blowing the horn and yelling, "Fuggin' bass-hole." According to Mom I was mimicking my father, who used to honk at aggressive drivers and yell, "Fucking asshole!" They say imitation is the highest form of flattery. Indeed Joseph Francis DeBlasi II was the apple of his father's eye.

The year 1969 held more unexpected and unprecedented events. The US put a man on the moon, the Mets skyrocketed from mediocrity to win the World Series, and Grandma Jennie moved the family out of Canarsie. She sold her parents' house, the only one she had ever lived in, and moved into a spectacular split-level in the exclusive Todt Hill section of Staten Island. Todt Hill has the distinction of being the highest point along the coast of the Eastern Seaboard, and from the huge bay window in Grandma Jennie's living room, we could see all of New Jersey.

Coincidentally that was also the year Uncle Mike knocked up his nineteen-year-old girlfriend, Kathy Smith. The predictable shotgun wedding followed, and Uncle Mike, Aunt Kathy and the baby moved into Grandma Jennie's house on the hill. Already second fiddle to her Joseph, the situation did nothing to help uncle Mike's standing in the family. Grandma Jennie's Joseph would never have gotten a girl pregnant out of wedlock! Just Uncle Mike's luck, Frank was born with jet-black hair. My grandfather was happy at least; he had finally gotten his Francis.

It was always my parents' intention to return to New York, and as soon as my father graduated from medical school, we did just that. My parents and I moved into the apartment downstairs from Grandpa Jack and Grandma Dar. As the first grandchild on both sides of the family, I received the royal treatment from many adoring relatives. That same year Mom's kid sister, Paula, married Jimmy, a scotch-drinking Irish cop. It might have been their wedding, but I stole the show in my little blue suit. My father carried me around the party as if I were God's gift to the world, much as he had been treated as a child. Grandma Jennie followed us around, saying, "*Que bella mi figlio*"—Italian for "what a beautiful son." Although she was referring to how cute I was, because of the direct translation and her adoration of Joseph Sr., everyone thought she was talking about him. It was a fair assumption.

I had so many toys, there was barely enough room for us in the apartment. Grandma Jennie wanted us to live with her, but the Todt Hill house was already bursting at the seams. She probably would have built an extension with her bare hands if my father asked her to, but it was easier for him to commute from Brooklyn to his internship at St. Vincent's Hospital in Manhattan. So we stayed in the cramped rooms, eking by on his meager intern's salary.

Money might have been tight, but no one outside the family would have known it, especially when, after becoming a resident at Maimonides Hospital in Brooklyn, my father went out and bought himself a Cadillac. The other residents at Maimonides must have thought he was a drug dealer; however, people in the neighborhood knew he was just a showy Sicilian with an indulgent mother. Most residents would be driving jalopies for the foreseeable future as they struggled under the weight of student loans, but not my father. Not wanting her Joseph to start out in a hole, Grandma Jennie had scrimped and saved to pay for his tuition outright.

This was what I would come to think of as my family's Camelot period. We were back in New York where we belonged, my father was finally a doctor, and my mother was pregnant with my brother, Stephen. The Paladinos and

DeBlasis celebrated every birthday and holiday together. Grandma Jennie's holiday parties were especially over the top. She and Great-Grandma Termini would start preparing days in advance, and the house on Todt Hill was filled with the smells of marinara sauce, cooking meats, and freshly baked pizza. To this day Grandma Dar says she never saw people who could cook and eat like the DeBlasis. My father and his brother, Mike, were called the "Piranha brothers" because they devoured every ravioli, meatball, and manicotti in sight, but Grandma Dar had another name for them. Watching the DeBlasis eat, she'd shake her head and say, "They're like wolves! Just when you think the feeding frenzy is over, out comes another course."

No one is really sure why, but around the time Stephen was born in August 1970, things began to fall apart. We had just moved to an apartment around the corner from Maimonides when Mom noticed that my father was spending less and less time at home. At first she attributed it to his having been made chief resident at the hospital. But there were other things that didn't add up. He was spending money foolishly, buying expensive clothing when he should have been saving money for his growing family. The strangest thing he bought was a pricey pair of cowboy boots that made him even taller than his six feet, four inches. "His behavior was bizarre," Mom said. "Something was definitely up."

Something was up all right—up half the skirts at Maimonides. Becoming a doctor had somehow transformed my father from a balding, red-haired giant into a hot commodity.

So long as he had that stethoscope dangling from his neck, there was some gold-digging nurse eager to grab the "howitzer" (as he fondly called it) dangling between his legs. To these women a doctor was fair game, no matter if he was married with two kids. Unfortunately it didn't matter to him either.

Somehow, in between his doctoring and his philandering, Dad still had the time and energy to father another child with my mom. On July 8, 1971, still blissfully ignorant of my father's cheating, she gave birth to their third son, Kevin. My father, however, did not share her enthusiasm; in fact early on in the pregnancy, he had floated the idea of an abortion, claiming they might not be able to afford a third child. Mom quickly sank that idea but failed to realize the true motive behind it: he wanted out of the marriage, and the last thing he needed was another baby to add to the child support.

Right before Christmas in 1971, my father finally confessed that he had not been playing cards with friends but had been carrying on a year-long affair with a nurse named Phyllis Valvano. A tall, leggy girl with long brown hair, Phyllis also worked at Maimonides. As he spilled the beans to my shocked and devastated mother, Joseph made it clear he was not seeking her forgiveness or even apologizing; instead he was blaming her. It was her fault, he insisted, that they had married so young and that he had not had the opportunity to date other women before he was tied down. He had conveniently forgotten that he had been the pursuer in the early days of their relationship and that he was the one who had pushed her to go steady. The days of him crying on Grandma Dar's doorstep were long gone.

As heartbreaking as his admission was and as crazy as his accusations were, my mother was not willing to give up so easily. She had been with him for twelve years, married for six, and they had three young boys. She wanted my brothers and me to grow up in an intact family, and at first my father agreed. But even as he was telling her that he wanted to stay married, he was also saying that he needed to sow his wild oats. He even suggested Mom should let him do his thing for a year or two, and then he would come back to her. To this day it makes my brothers and me sick that she was treated with such disrespect; however, as we would soon learn, this was only the tip of the iceberg.

A few months later, in February 1972, my parents took the three of us to Florida on a trip they had booked the summer before. It was there that Dad told Mom, "Whether you like it or not, I'm leaving you." As if that weren't enough, he added, "My whole life I have gotten everything I want. Now I want to be free to screw other women."

In an effort to make my mother angry enough to ask for a divorce, he told her that in addition to Phyllis Valvano, there had been several other conquests including a *shvatza* nurse. In fact, he told her, it was Phyllis who had suggested a name for his youngest child. "Phyllis liked the professional basketball player Kevin Lockery, and she told me if I have another son, I should name him Kevin." And so he had.

When my mother still didn't take the bait, he accused her of having an affair, and even insinuated Kevin wasn't his child. Even my father must have known how ridiculous this sounded because, aside from the obvious reason that my mother was a loving and faithful wife, Kevin looked exactly like him. My father would later concede that Kevin was his son but referred to him as "the hole in the scumbag."

My father's personality had changed so radically that my mother was worried he had a brain tumor. "It was as if my husband had walked out one day, and someone else who looked just like him walked in." Years later, after she had witnessed my mania for the first time, she told me it was scary how much my behavior resembled my father's at the time of the divorce.

Today there is no doubt in my mom's mind that my father is manic. But back then she had never even heard of bipolar disorder let alone had any inkling that her eldest son's life would be irreparably damaged by it. All she knew was that her marriage was over and that she would be raising three young sons on her own. She cried the whole plane ride home from Florida, and on April 1, 1972, Joseph officially left his wife and children and took an apartment on Staten Island. His parting words to the woman he had once adored was, "You can have the boys for now, but when they're older they'll want to live with their father." Camelot had officially gone bye-bye.

CHAPTER 2

Hatchet Job

My father used his new Staten Island digs more for storage than as a home; in truth he was spending most of his time at Grandma Jennie's house on Todt Hill. When my mother heard the news, she was angry and a little surprised. Grandma Jennie had always spoiled her son rotten, but now he was a grown man with children of his own. In Mom's opinion the right thing for Grandma Jennie to do was tell him, "Go back to your wife and babies, or don't ever talk to me again."

Like *that* was going to happen. Sure, my grandmother was sick over the fact that her son had left three beautiful babies in diapers, but she wasn't going to give him an ultimatum she couldn't stick with. Just as she had tried to convince him not to get serious with my mother when they were dating, she tried to convince him to return home. However, she was met with the same steely refusal. He wasn't going back, and there was nothing she could say or do about it.

Like Frankenstein, Grandma Jennie had created a monster, and now even she couldn't control him. So maybe her Joseph wasn't perfect after all, but he was still a doctor and still her son. The rest of the DeBlasi family also immediately closed ranks behind him. My parents' divorce didn't just affect them or my brothers and me; it created a toxic ripple effect throughout both sides of the family.

Today divorce may be as common as a cockroach in a Brooklyn apartment building, and kids with happily married parents are more the exception than the rule. It's not uncommon to hear about divorced couples who socialize with each other, attend each other's second or third weddings, and even help care for their former in-laws. But this was back in 1972, when divorce was still a dirty word particularly for Catholics, although I don't think it would have mattered when my parents broke up. The family still would have been in an uproar. While the rest of society may have, for better or worse, changed its social mores, one segment of the population remains firmly entrenched in the Brooklyn Dodger days: Italian-Americans.

So while Grandma Jennie was looking forward to having her Joseph around the house again, she was certainly not looking forward to the humiliation of having a divorced son. She worried what impression people would have of him and the entire family when they heard the news. What would the pastry-eating bishop think of the DeBlasis now that her Joseph had defiled one of the institutions of the Roman Catholic Church?

She knew, of course, that there was no hope of keeping it a secret; she still had plenty of friends and family in Canarsie, and the gossip pipeline between Staten Island and Brooklyn was going strong. Desperate for some damage control, the DeBlasis began badmouthing my mother all over town. "Joseph isn't the bad guy here," they'd tell whoever would listen. "That Regina's a real *putana*."

When word of the smear campaign reached the Paladinos, the situation almost came to violence. The normally mild-mannered Grandpa Jack, already devastated by Joseph's treatment of his daughter and three grandsons, lost it when he heard the DeBlasis were calling her a whore. His younger brother, Guido, intercepted Grandpa Jack on his way to Maimonides, where he was headed with a hatchet to kill my father. Uncle Guido convinced him that his grandsons would be worse off without a dad—even a lousy one—not to mention the fact that Jack would be charged with murder. The prospect of jail did not bother Grandpa Jack as much as the thought of Grandpa Frank being the only father figure left in his grandsons' lives.

Around that time Grandma Dar began receiving prank phone calls, which she attributed to somebody in the DeBlasi camp. It had become an Italian version of the Hatfields and the McCoys. Having come from such a warm, loving family, Grandma Dar had been particularly devastated by the breakup of my parents' marriage. What she really couldn't understand was how the DeBlasis, who had known my mother since she was a girl, could turn on her so viciously, especially after what Joseph had done.

"They were awful to your mother, just awful," Grandma Dar told my brothers and me. Having witnessed some of the DeBlasis' behavior, we didn't find this difficult to believe. We were, however, shocked to hear that the usually reserved Grandma Dar had told Grandma Jennie, "You should flush your head down the toilet."

These were dark days for the Paladinos, but no one had it harder than my mother. Within a few short months, her entire life—or, at least, the illusion of it—had imploded. She had gone from the wife of a doctor she had helped put through medical school to a twenty-nine-year-old divorcee with three children under the age of five, two of them still in diapers. She had no money, no job, and, since my father had taken his big flashy Caddy with him, no car. They had given my Grandpa Frank their old '66 Chevy Impala a few years earlier, and when my mother called him to ask for it back he not only refused but told her not to call the house anymore. My mother had lost not only her husband but his entire family. To the DeBlasis she had simply ceased to exist.

Sometimes it seems like we had all ceased to exist for my father as well. One time there was an extended blackout in the neighborhood. As we sat in the dark, nervous and wondering when the electricity would come back on, we saw neither hide nor hair of my father. He didn't even call to see if we were okay. Instead we relied on the kindness of a neighbor who walked me down five flights of stairs to put me on the bus to

Peter Pan Nursery School while my mother watched Stephen and Kevin.

Never a big drinker, mom was so despondent one evening that she almost drank herself to death. But being a mother was the most important thing to her, so she knew she had to keep going for our sakes. With the help of Grandma Dar and Grandpa Jack, she did the best she could to make a new life for us, but it was far from easy.

Thanks to Grandpa Frank, she now had to do all our shopping on foot, which, with three little kids, was nothing short of a nightmare. She would put Stephen and Kevin in a stroller and push them with one hand while holding on to my meaty little fist with the other.

One hot summer day, Mom returned from a long shopping trip with two large grocery bags in her hands and the three of us in tow. That same kind neighbor was standing outside, her lips tight as she looked at us. "I'm sorry to tell you this, honey," she said, pointing to my brother Stephen, "but your kid is missing a shoe."

Not in a financial position to replace it, my mom and I trekked all the way back to the store to look for it while the neighbor stayed with Stephen and Kevin. We finally found the tiny sandal in the diaper aisle. Who could blame Mom for hitting the Jack Daniels that night? "If not for Grandma and Grandpa's help," she's told me more than once, "I never would have survived to take care of you boys."

Luckily my grandparents were in a position to help us out financially. In the 1960s Grandma Dar had returned to work as a seamstress in a garment factory. As long as she had dinner on the table by six, Grandpa Jack was okay with her working. Now the extra money was our saving grace. In addition to helping Mom out with grocery bills and babysitting costs, Grandpa Jack bought her a used green 1970 Chevy Malibu. Even all these years later, I can still remember how hard it was to shut the door on that car.

I can also recall other things from that time in my childhood, in 1972-1973. Psychiatrists have suggested that as the oldest child, I remember my parents together, happily married, and that the divorce affected me more than it did my brothers. But to my way of thinking, this theory does little to explain my mental illness because I have absolutely no recollection of my father's ever having lived with Mom. Actually my first clear childhood memory is of Stephen climbing out of his crib, crouching down, and relieving himself right on the floor. Who could forget a thing like that? Stephen's failed potty training exercise took place sometime in the early fall of 1972. I was not yet four years old, and my father was long gone.

My parents' divorce became final in April 1973 after a year of separation. During that time my father had taken a job as an emergency room doctor. ER doctors typically make less than other physicians, which resulted in low alimony and child support: fifty dollars a week and thirty-three dollars a week per kid. My mother's suspicion that he had taken a low-paying job for this purpose was confirmed when, soon after the judge's decree, he left the ER job and, along with a partner, opened his own practice. When we also learned that he had conveniently waited to move the rest of his things into Grandma Jennie's house, everything fell into place. He had been paying for that apartment only to show the court that he did not have that much disposable income to pay alimony. Once that matter was settled, he didn't need the apartment anymore, and he could return fully to the DeBlasi fold where he belonged.

CHAPTER 3

PWP

Right around the time my father was moving those fancy cowboy boots out of his apartment, we were evicted from ours. We had been living in a place provided by Maimonides Hospital because my father was a resident. Now that he was no longer a resident, they kicked us out. The judge had ordered him to pay our rent up to $325 a month, so Mom set out to find a suitable place for us to live—not an easy task when you have three little kids and a limited budget. One landlady on Ocean Avenue told her she had hoped to rent to someone without infants. My mom just smiled at her and said, "That's okay. I was hoping to rent a nicer place."

Eventually Mom did find a nicer apartment on the top floor of a three-story brick row house on Paerdegat Fifteenth Street in Canarsie. We lived right above the landlord, an Italian man named Mr. Vecchio. Married with four children and a Costa Rican maid named Mimi, Mr. Vecchio was a kindhearted family man who had a soft spot for my mother and our situation. Knowing that my father took his time in sending the support money each month, he never said anything when we were late with the rent. This made him a considerate human being. The fact that he put up with our small but active feet constantly stomping around right over his head made him a saint.

While our mother was still reeling from my father's defection, she knew that life had to go on. For her this meant staying strong for us and deciding what she was going to do with the rest of her life. For my brothers and me, it meant getting into as much mischief as possible, usually at the Vecchios' expense. As we would soon learn, even saints run out of patience every now and again.

When I was about six, my brothers and I started playing this game we called Mean Joe Green. I would wear my green pajamas and run around the island in the kitchen. Stephen and Kevin's goal was to tackle me before I could make it around the island and back. We loved that game and played it until we inevitably heard Mr. Vecchio's broomstick violently pounding against his ceiling. But he never held a grudge; the next time he saw us, he'd be offering us money to pull weeds in the backyard.

He would have lost it if he knew some of the other things my brothers and I were up to. Always on the hunt for some new activity, we decided one night to cut our way through the floor so we could spy on the Vecchios below. Like most hardwood flooring, it had these very narrow spaces between some of the planks. As the oldest I ran the entire operation.

"Get the knife," I'd whisper, and my brothers would creep silently into the kitchen, get a blade, and deliver it to me. I would then jab it into one particularly large crack between two planks. To avoid detection, capture, and severe punishment, we created an elaborate signal system. Kevin would stand guard near Mom's bedroom while Stephen took the post down the hall, where he could see both Kevin and me. Should Mom emerge from her bedroom, Kevin would signal to Steve, and Steve would alert me to stop the cutting and hide the knife. It was extremely effective. In all the years the three of us lived there together, Mom didn't catch us once. However, no matter how much I cut, we never seemed to make any headway.

When we weren't playing Mean Joe Green or attempting to renovate the Vecchios' house, my brothers and I were actually very well behaved. Mom learned early on that if she was going to raise three boys on her own, she had to be strict, and to this end she developed her own brand of behavior modification. When we were still little enough to go in a playpen, she'd set it up in front of the television and leave us there for hours. It worked like a charm because when she did finally let us out, we were so mesmerized by the boob tube that we'd just move over to the couch and continue watching. Mr. Rogers was such a constant presence in our house that we thought he actually lived with us. I guess we were looking for a father figure.

The only time we got up off the couch was when we heard the booming voice of the broadcaster say, "This is a public service announcement. Please stand by." The three of us, used to obeying commands, would get up and literally "stand by" right next to the television. The rare laugh it elicited from our exhausted, shell-shocked mother inspired us to continue doing it long after we stopped taking the broadcaster's announcement literally.

There were times, of course, when Mr. Rogers wasn't enough to keep us in line, and thanks to my father's sudden defection from the family, Mom had to develop a bag of tricks on the fly. Like a lot of Italian mothers, screaming was a favorite.

"Ma, don't yell," we'd plead, cupping our hands over our ears. "Just hit us."

Mom wasn't much for corporal punishment, but she sometimes resorted to pinching if we really crossed the line. She'd run up to the offending child and, with her thumb and pointer finger, grab the fleshy part of the arm and tug. She'd probably still be pinching us today if she hadn't read a magazine article that claimed pinching causes cancer. We never knew whether the study had any scientific merit, but we sure were grateful for it.

Later Mom became more innovative. Hot Wheels made a toy with long, thin, flexible plastic tracks that doubled nicely as whips. The sound of them whooshing through the air was almost worse than the pain they inflicted or the ugly red welts that appeared a few seconds later. No matter what mischief we were engaged in, if we heard, "That's it! I'm getting the whip!" we stopped in our tracks.

The most important thing to Mom was keeping things as normal as possible for my brothers and me; she never wanted us to know what she was going through. She was learning to be a single parent and a divorcée at the same time, both of which involved grieving the future she had envisioned with our father. The fact that he had run around with other women during their marriage had really done a job on her self-esteem. And, to add insult to injury, she was also dealing with the loss of the DeBlasi family, who had been a part of her life since she was a teenager. Between that and taking care of us, she needed a break by the time Friday rolled around. Thankfully Grandma Dar was more than happy to take us off her hands for the weekend.

To my brothers and me, staying at our grandparents' was as good as a vacation to Disney World. We had our own room there with two single beds for Stephen and me. Kevin slept between us on a cot that Grandma Dar kept in the basement when we weren't around. Every other Friday my mom would pull the Malibu up in front of the Paladinos' brick house; then, while she went in to say hello to her parents, my brothers and I would sneak down into the basement and get the cot. When we suddenly appeared in the kitchen, Grandma would throw out her hands and say, "What are *you* doing here?" as if she'd never expected to see us.

Grandma Dar always had something for us to do. She'd set up a bowling alley in the back bedroom using these giant cardboard spools that she brought home from work as pins. At night, if we were good, she'd let us watch *S.W.A.T.*, one of those cheesy cop shows the '70s are famous for. When we knew it was coming on, we were all pleases and thank yous and "May I please be excused from the table, Grandma?" One false move would have her exclaiming, "This is for the birds!" Once you heard her talking about the birds, you knew you had gone too far.

Grandpa Jack, who by that time had been diagnosed with Parkinson's disease, took a less active role in our visits. Basically he liked to feed us peaches that had been soaking in wine; that way he knew we'd be knocked out by the time he went to bed. My brothers and I would savor the super-sweet fruit, not to mention the relaxed, woozy feeling that mysteriously overtook us afterward. Sometimes we were lucky just to make it to *S.W.A.T.*

At bedtime Grandma Dar would go through her whole shocked routine again when she found the cot all set up in the spare bedroom. "How did *this* get up here?" We had to be pretty dumb to think she didn't hear us banging and rattling the cot up the metal-edged basement steps weekend after weekend.

While we were getting drunk off peaches and playing spool-pin bowling, Mom was slowly rebuilding her life. Once the initial shock of the divorce wore off and we were settled in a decent home, she took a solo trip to Europe. It was an extremely brave thing for a newly divorced woman who had never travelled alone before. This trip went a long way toward repairing the damage my father's serial cheating had done. She wasn't complaining when she said, "The men in Italy were like hounds chasing after me—and everything else with two legs."

In fact it was almost a letdown when she got back to the States and men weren't whistling at her everywhere she went.

Their overtures may have been more subtle, but American men paid Mom plenty of attention when she went out on the weekends. A few tactless relatives had told her it would be hard to find a man willing to date a woman with children, but she soon proved them wrong. She was a young, very attractive woman, and even after three kids had kept her trim figure. She was quite a catch, and when she joined Parents without Partners (PWP), the men lined up to ask her out. Knowing we loved to bowl at Grandma Dar's, she signed us up for the PWP bowling league. Every other Saturday we got to show off our skills with a bunch of other divorced parents and their kids. It was a lot of fun except for the men who offered bowling tips in a rather lame attempt to impress our mother. My brothers and I were semi-pros by that time and didn't need their advice. Mom probably thought it was awkward to flirt in front of us, so she just offered them a polite thank you and left it at that.

In 1974 one man at PWP did catch Mom's eye. David Karmi, a slight, Jewish man thirteen years her senior, was completely different from our father. In fact he was different from anyone she had ever known. David stood only five feet, five inches with a wiry build and a cleft chin. Born in Transylvania, Romania, David had survived the concentration camp that took his parents. After the war he arrived in the US with nothing but the shirt on his back, yet he still managed to make a fortune in the construction business. David was also divorced with kids, but they were much older than we were.

Kind and caring, David loved to pamper my mother with

gifts and dinners. He even took her on vacations around the world. What really won her over, though, was that he included me, Kevin, and Stephen on their dates. On the Saturday nights we didn't spend at Grandma Dar's, David would take us all to Cookies Steakhouse. Cookies may have been known for its prime rib, but my brothers and I loved it for the peel-n-eat shrimp and dessert bar. With the measly thirty-three dollars in child support our father provided, we did not get much of either at home.

We felt so at ease around David that we probably would have asked him about his experience in the concentration camps if Mom hadn't warned us about it. "David does not like to talk about what happened in the war," Mom told us, afraid we would embarrass her and upset him. "So don't ask him about it." We obeyed, but it was hard to stop scanning his body for the tattooed numbers that our father told us he probably had as a camp survivor.

One night after we stuffed ourselves on shrimp at Cookies, David and Mom took us to see *The Kentucky Fried Movie*. They must not have noticed that it was rated R for profanity and nudity, otherwise they never would have taken us. Mom spent the next two hours telling us to cover our eyes and our ears. For weeks afterward six-year-old Kevin kept reciting one of the lines: "Christ, did a cow shit in here?" Knowing it was her fault, Mom didn't even threaten the whip. She just laughed.

Most of the time, David planned more kid-appropriate activities. He took us to a Mets double header even though he wasn't a fan; he spent the first game reading the Sunday *Times* and the second game napping. He introduced us to skiing and tennis and even took us all on vacation to Lake George. The night before we left, my brothers and I were so excited we couldn't get to sleep. It was only after we heard Mom say, "One more sound and I get the whip" that we finally settled down.

CHAPTER 4

Shangri-La

The DeBlasis may have divorced themselves from Mom, but they still considered my brothers and me very much part of the family. When my father walked out, the family court judge granted him weekend visitation, and although we loved living with our mother, every other Friday found us with our noses pressed up against the window as we waited for a glimpse of his Caddy rolling up the block. In reality, though, we didn't see much of him on these visits, because between his rounds at the hospital and his affairs with Phyllis Valvano and others, our father's weekends were very hectic. It was really his mother, Grandma Jennie, who took care of us, and it was a task she was only too happy to undertake. No matter who watched us, the moment we crossed the Verrazano Bridge onto Staten Island, it was like we had crossed into a different family and a completely different life.

By 1973, after having another son, Uncle Mike and Aunt Kathy had finally moved out of Grandma Jennie's house and into a place of their own. Still the house was full to overflowing with several generations of boisterous DeBlasis under one roof. Our father was living there, as were Great-Grandpa (Pop) and Great-Grandma Termini. Even Grandma Jennie's brother, Michael, who everyone called by his initials, MRT (Raymond was his middle name), moved in after his first marriage ended. By that time all the bedrooms were taken, and he was forced to sleep on a pull-out couch in the living room. For six long years he opened that sofa bed up at night and closed it in the morning. In 1976 he remarried and moved out, but to this day my brothers and I still refer to any sofa bed as an "MRT."

With six adults (sometimes seven if our father brought a girlfriend around) fawning over us, even Grandma Dar's house couldn't compete with our weekends on Staten Island. There was no bedtime or wine-laden peaches; we stayed up until 3:00 a.m. eating ice cream, drinking sodas, and watching the adults play cards. Then we'd pile in three to a bed and awake at our leisure to a feast of French toast, eggs, bacon, orange juice, milk, and Flintstones vitamins. Grandma Jennie was perpetually worried that Mom was not feeding us enough.

We'd spend the day playing with toys in the den or ball in the backyard, and we were never quite able to figure out how Grandma Jennie and Great-Grandma Termini could manage to be in the kitchen cooking and still keep a watchful eye on us. If they weren't around, Grandpa Frank, Pop, or the MRT looked on, and, like all children would, we basked in the attention. We also loved the brand-new clothes, toys, and baseball equipment Grandma Jennie kept for us. She even let us keep pet frogs there, which was surprising given her notorious fear of germs. Her only condition was that we wear these huge mittens whenever we handled them. It was ridiculous, but knowing we had a good thing going, we didn't argue the point.

We were catered to from the minute we walked in the door on Friday night to the minute we left late on Sunday. We'd walk back into the apartment in Canarsie carrying bags of bubble gum and candy, which we'd set down before our mother grabbed us into a fierce hug.

While everyday at Grandma Jennie's may have seemed like Christmas, it was nothing compared to the real deal—the traditional Italian Christmas Eve feast with every kind of seafood known to man and a dinner table that seemed to stretch for miles. Grandma Jennie served jumbo shrimp that blew Cookies' away, always making sure they were peeled to perfection for us. As for the desserts, just imagine walking into your favorite Italian bakery and eating whatever you wanted. There were trays of syrupy *sfingi* balls, almond cookies, and *sfogliatelles*; and, of course, *pastachiotti*, the cream-filled pastries that were my father's favorite, were always in abundance. Even among Staten Island Italians, Grandma Jennie's Christmas Eve spread stood out.

After Uncle Mike and Aunt Kathy arrived with their young sons, Frankie and Michael, we'd consume course after incredible course until we were ready to burst. Around midnight all the kids were herded into one of the bedrooms with an adult—usually Aunt Kathy—standing guard. Inevitably one of us would yell, "Look! There's Santa!" and point out the window, across the water at the twinkling lights of Elizabeth, New Jersey. The rest of us would rush to the window, all swearing we saw the sleigh sailing through the clouds, about to hang a turn toward Staten Island. From the living room we'd hear a couple of deep "ho ho ho's" and jingling bells followed by grunts and groans—the sounds of the adults hauling the presents out of their hiding places.

"Don't go out," Aunt Kathy would say when she saw us eyeing the bedroom door, "or Santa's not gonna leave any presents."

After what felt like an eternity, Aunt Kathy (acting on some mysterious cue from the other room) would open the door, moving aside so as not to be trampled by screaming kids racing out to the living room. We'd find it literally covered with gifts on the floor, under the twelve-foot Christmas tree—even on the MRT's sofa bed. Some were impeccably wrapped; other bigger presents like bicycles and Big Wheels were adorned only with dangling festive tickets that had some lucky DeBlasi boys' names on them. My brothers and cousins and I would stand there in shock, savoring the moment before diving in. It was a euphoria that remained unparalleled until I experienced my first mania nearly two decades later.

We got everything from baseball bats and catchers' mitts to clothes and board games; the presents were endless. After every box was opened and every piece of wrapping paper discarded, Uncle Mike and Aunt Kathy would finally take their boys home. Frankie and Michael were always happy with their presents but must have wondered why Santa always seemed to bring their cousins bigger and better things. Eventually they'd realize that just like their father had played second fiddle to "my Joseph," they would play second fiddle to Kevin, and Stephen and me. This, coupled with the fact that our father was a doctor and therefore had more money to spend on presents, meant that there would always be a smaller take for them on Todt Hill. For Frankie and Michael, this had to be worse than finding out there was no Santa Claus.

My brothers and I had already figured out that being "my Joseph's" sons made us the favorites with Grandma Jennie and Grandpa Frank. It's not that they didn't love Frankie and Michael, it was just plain to see that they loved us a little more. Even the MRT was biased in our favor. A car salesman by trade, he could spin a tale for hours. Although he had never served in the armed forces, he loved to tell stories about "the war," often inserting all five of Grandma Jennie's grandsons as the main characters. Inevitably each story ended with my brothers and me capturing the "Japs" while Frankie and Michael were relegated to the back lines to carry the pots and pans. It seemed unfair at the time, but when we got older it dawned on us that the MRT may have told the same stories to our cousins only featuring them as the heroes. Since he could sell ice to Eskimos and sand to Arabs, we didn't put it past him.

Some people might have stopped at telling war stories,

but not the MRT. He was like a fifty-year-old kid—he had the carefree attitude of a child coupled with the means and opportunities of an adult. One Friday night we arrived at Grandma Jennie's to find he had bought each of us a toy cap gun. Always overprotective of her boys, Grandma Jennie wasn't keen on the idea but wasn't going to be the bad guy, especially when she saw the looks on our faces. She told us we could play with them the next day, which, to three boys chomping at the bit, might as well have been next year.

The next morning my brothers and I got up at the crack of dawn and crept into the living room. Everyone else in the house was still asleep—everyone but the MRT, who was just closing his sofa bed. He grabbed the guns then led us, still in our pajamas, to the yard, where the four of us acted out our version of the Battle of the Bulge. We never found out who won, though, because Grandma Jennie called a cease-fire.

"Are you nuts? Letting the boys out without coats and shoes? I ought to strangle you!"

We stopped shooting and looked up at the second-floor balcony. Grandma Jennie might have been wearing a muumuu and curlers, but she still was as tough as Patton.

Without hesitation the MRT looked up at his big sister and calmly responded, "But Jenn, if this was a real war, the boys wouldn't have had time to put on their coats and shoes."

While our father was too busy to spend much time with us at the house, he—along with Grandma Jennie and Grandpa Frank—did take us on vacation to Chicago. The Graffeos, distant relatives who had treated him well while he was in med school, lived out there, and we owed them a visit. It was 1975, and Dad had traded in the Caddy for a brand-new white Lincoln Continental. The six of us piled in, and we hit the road, listening for most of the ride to Jim Croce, who my father loved. I think "Bad, Bad Leroy Brown" played through most of Pennsylvania. When we finally got to Chicago twelve hours later, my father and grandfather dragged the luggage out of the trunk. We had extra suitcases filled with the pillowcases, sheets, and towels from home. Grandma Jennie wasn't taking any chances with hotel linens.

My brothers and I spent much of that week as we did on Staten Island: staying up late, playing hearts, watching television, and eating. We had dinner at the Graffeos' one night, but the Italian sausages Mrs. Graffeo made were too spicy for us kids. After we left their house, Grandma Jennie insisted on treating us to a lobster dinner. We each ordered a lobster except for Grandpa Frank, who said, "I'll just eat what the boys don't finish." Well, he ended up ordering room service that night because, much to Grandma Jennie's delight, we consumed everything but the shells.

Our father had been happy and relaxed all week, but when it came time to head back to New York, he was suddenly hell bent on making good time. Grandma Jennie kept telling him to slow down, but he ignored her, keeping the pedal to the metal and the Lincoln speeding at over eighty miles an hour. We made it to Ohio before we saw the flashing lights of a state trooper behind us. My father pulled over and offered the trooper his most genial smile. The trooper didn't smile back.

Much to my father's surprise, he wasn't impressed by the MD license plates, and the fact that he was speeding with three small children in the car only made the infraction worse.

My father was still shocked that he couldn't talk his way out of it when the cop delivered more good news: because we were from out of state and doing twenty-five miles over the speed limit, Dad had to go to court and pay the ticket *that day*. Used to getting his way, "my Joseph" was fuming, and it only got worse when, after pulling up to the courthouse, he stepped his size-twelve Buster Brown right onto a big pile of dog shit.

Furious, he scraped his shoe against the curb and disappeared into the building, leaving the rest of us to sit in the sweltering Lincoln for the next three hours. While he was gone, Grandma Jennie had plenty to say. Apparently he had been driving like a lunatic because he was in a rush to get back to Rita, some new nurse he had met at the hospital. As it turned out it, it wouldn't be the only time our father stepped in shit, then left the rest of us behind to deal with the mess.

Whether we spent the weekend away or at Grandma Jennie's house, returning to Brooklyn on Sunday nights was a sobering event. Still on a sugar high from all the M&Ms and Dixie ice cream cups we had devoured, we kissed our adoring fans good-bye and headed back to Mom. On those nights our father drove much more slowly than usual, making the already depressing trip seem like a funeral procession. He used the extra time with us to state his case, saying things like, "I left your mother in the divorce, not you three boys" or how the four of us could be like *My Three Sons* and the MRT could be our Uncle Charlie.

Other than that he didn't speak too much about Mom, but he didn't stop us from talking about her either. We had told him the story of how David and Mom went to a costume party for Halloween. Mom went as a Playboy Bunny, and David was so small in stature that he was able to borrow my Cub Scout uniform. He wore his own pants, but the shirt fit him like a glove. Mom would always tell us that despite his size, David was incredibly strong, maybe even stronger than our father. Kevin let that part slip on one of our weekends at Grandma Jennie's and unwittingly set off one of the famous Dad tirades. "That little Jew, stronger than me? I *crap* bigger than him. I'd crush him like a grape!" Even though he no longer wanted Mom, it surely zinged his ego to hear she had survived and was happily dating another man.

But mostly he told us stories about his childhood, particularly how Grandma Jennie had made him study all the time. He recounted the long hours he had spent at his desk doing homework while his cousins, Frank Sardinia and Anthony Lapadulo, were out breaking streetlights with a slingshot. At the time he resented his mother for being strict; like most boys his age, he'd rather have been jerking around with his cousins instead of cooped up in the house with a pile of books. But he sure was grateful to his mother now because there he was, a doctor, while his cousins were breaking their backs landscaping.

"You three better study hard too," he told us. "You don't want to end up pitching watermelons your whole life." Whatever he told us, we soaked up like little sponges. He was funny, passionate, and, at six foot four and two-hundred and fifty pounds, quite intimidating.

After getting off the Belt Parkway, we'd make him circle our block half a dozen times then pick up speed on Paerdegat Fourteenth Street so we could fly over the bumps like we were on a roller coaster. Sure it was fun, but mostly we didn't want the weekend to end.

Inevitably we'd find ourselves in front of the Vecchios' house. Then, to make sure we didn't fall on the cement steps, Dad would carry each one of us up the long stoop, proclaiming, "I's got you, baby." At the door he'd kiss us good-bye—big sloppy, wet kisses. He always said good-bye to me last, telling me to look out for Kevin and Stephen because I was the man of the house. Then, with a sorrowful expression, he'd climb back into the Lincoln and pull away. We waved until he turned the corner and was out of sight. Then Mom would let us in and, as painful as it must have been for her, ask to hear all about our weekend.

Each Sunday night our father dropped off three very conflicted children. We loved our mother, and we loved living in Canarsie. We had a hundred kids to play with on our block, and just around the corner there was Seaview Park, where we played little league. We caught toads at the "frog tree" in the park, and Mom let us keep them as pets. I was a Cub Scout, and, since Mom was a den mother, Mr. Rosenhouse, the den leader, often let Stephen and Kevin tag along on our adventures. We enjoyed going to Grandma Dar's house to bowl and watch *S.W.A.T.* We went to Riis Park beach and even belonged to a pool club called the Brook. When it rained, we always had Mean Joe Green and our secret floor renovations to occupy us.

Our childhood in Canarsie would have been pretty close to perfect if not for one thing: nothing could compare to the Shangri-La experience of Todt Hill. How could Mom, with her strict parenting, 7:30 p.m. bedtimes, early school mornings, evening homework, and tight money ever compete with the carnival atmosphere of Grandma Jennie's? The answer was she couldn't. Mom knew this, and, more importantly, so did our father.

CHAPTER 5

The Big Freckled Fist

It started out as a joke—our father banging his big freckled fist on Grandma Jennie's kitchen table with all of us cheering him on. Then he would chant in a deep, halting voice, "Tell… the…judge…you…want…to…live…with…your…father…. Your father…. Your father." He would repeat this—half joking, half serious—the whole night. In 1972, when he had told Mom that he would eventually get custody of us, it had seemed like a pipe dream. Back then, absent extreme circumstances, it was unheard of for any father to get custody of his children, let alone a single father who worked long hours at his medical practice.

By 1976, however, he and Rita, the nurse he'd risked our lives for on the drive back from Chicago, had been going hot and heavy for over a year. For the first time since the divorce, he was dating someone he considered marriage material. Early in the relationship, they had gone on a double date with Uncle Mike and Aunt Kathy. When our father asked Uncle Mike what he thought of her, Mike offered his version of the thumbs-up. He took in Rita's shapely five-foot-seven frame and said, "She has some freakin' body."

Rita was raised in Old Forge, Pennsylvania, a coalmining town outside Scranton. She had just separated from her first husband when she met our father. The story goes that her first husband, who was Jewish, had initiated the separation because his family would not accept Rita, a non-Jew. She often showed up for her shift at Maimonides in tears. She was devastated, she told coworkers, but apparently not so devastated that she couldn't start a relationship with Dr. DeBlasi soon after.

Rita had passed muster with Uncle Mike; however, this wouldn't prove so easy when it came to Grandma Jennie. By that time my grandmother had once again become the central figure in her Joseph's life; she had also become a weekend mother to my brothers and me, and she had no desire to relinquish either role. Our father insinuated that Grandma Jennie wanted him to get custody of us but never remarry; that way she would get to raise us. Whatever the case Grandma Jennie wasn't too keen on this coalminer's daughter coming into her family, "thinking who she was."

However, she found a pretty formidable foe in Rita, who had already been burned by in-laws in the past. Rita was determined to show Grandma Jennie that she was not going to be cowed. The problem was Grandma Jennie had invented cowed, especially when it came to her Joseph. Needless to say their relationship got off to an inauspicious start.

Despite Grandma Jennie's reservations, our father and Rita were married on September 4, 1976. Not only did her Joseph marry a woman she wasn't fond of, but he had gotten her pregnant out of wedlock. The wedding was a grand affair at the Todt Hill Country Club, and eight months and seven days later my half brother Frank was born. At least this time our father picked the name. With Rita's arrival, Phyllis Valvano, the woman who had suggested the name Kevin for my brother, moved to Florida, and our new stepmother had the sense to go along with the Italian tradition. But she was still in Grandma Jennie's doghouse for other reasons, the biggest being that she had convinced our father to move out of the house on Todt Hill and purchase a new one in the Grasmere section of Staten Island. Not only did it mean less time with her Joseph, but it also meant he would no longer be bringing us to Todt Hill on the weekends.

On the Friday night immediately following their honeymoon, Grandma Jennie called the new house to inquire if we had arrived. She and Grandpa Frank wanted to come over and see us. Rita had answered the phone and told Grandma Jennie she couldn't see us until Sunday, as Rita and our father had made other plans.

To Grandma Jennie this was a slap in the face. "*You* don't tell *me*," she said coldly, "when I can and cannot see my own grandchildren." Fearing a major rift, our father brokered a compromise. We saw Grandma Jennie that Saturday night.

As we would later learn, our father had very specific moti-
vations for keeping the peace between his mother and his new
wife. In addition to preserving his sanity, he needed them
both in order to get custody of his three boys. He needed Rita
onboard because no judge was going to give him custody if he
were single. He needed Grandma Jennie because buying the
new house had wiped him out, and he knew she would give
him the funds necessary to fight what lawyers were telling him
would be a long, dirty, and expensive custody battle. He would
have to turn Mom into the villain just as he'd done during
the divorce, and for this Rita and Grandma Jennie had to put
aside their differences and present a united front. As funny
as it seemed at the time, he wasn't kidding when he slammed
his freckled fist onto the table and chanted. Like he had told
Mom on that trip to Florida, he always got what he wanted,
and he wanted custody of his sons. If she were devastated all
over again, so be it.

With all his ducks lined up, he now took to pounding his
big, freckled fist on the kitchen table in Grasmere. "Tell the
judge you want to live with your father.... Your father." The
fist was pounding with more and more frequency, and by the
time Frank was born in May 1977, the brainwashing was in
full swing. Dad began referring to our mother as "the cunt
from Canarsie" and said the only reason she wanted us was for
the child support. None the wiser, Mom played right into his
hands when he came to get us on Friday nights. She'd yell at
him about the checks being late. He screamed back, accusing

her of spending the child support on herself. My brothers and I heard it all.

One time the fighting got so loud that Mimi downstairs had the phone in her hand, ready to call 911. Sobbing with anger and frustration, Mom threw a bag of children's clothes at Dad to show where the support checks were going. The bag ripped as she threw it, and all the clothes came cascading down the steps. My brothers and I, shaken, scurried to pick them up. They still had the store tags on. As soon as we got into the Lincoln, our father repeated that Mom just wanted us for the support payments. Although we had just picked up a bag full of brand-new clothes costing at least $75, we believed him. We believed whatever he told us.

CHAPTER 6

Taxi?

As the oldest I was the most susceptible to my father's manipulations. Nothing made me feel better than making him proud of me, and nothing made him prouder than hearing me say bad things about Mom. Under his careful coaching, I started complaining to Mom that she wasn't spending all the child support on us. After hearing this a dozen times, she finally told me to put my money where my mouth was. She gave me my share of the child support—$33.33 for the week—and told me to see how well I did with it. The next day I was pushing my own shopping cart around the grocery store to pick up milk, butter, eggs, and whatever else I liked to eat. When it came time to pay for a Cub Scout trip, I was broke. When I told my father how fast the money had gone, he dismissed it. Mom had cheated me, he said, by making me buy my own food instead of giving her a certain percentage of the cost of a loaf of bread, a gallon of milk, et cetera. At the age of nine, my mother had me paying for my groceries, and my father was lecturing me on economics. Things were starting to get messy.

As if that weren't enough, our new stepmother started putting her two cents into the mix. When we arrived at their house on Friday nights, Rita would grumble that our fingernails were dirty and we were not bathed properly. Then she'd drag us off, one at time, to wash our hair in the kitchen sink and cut our fingernails, often so short that they hurt. After the grooming we'd have a late dinner and play cards or Monopoly until the wee hours of the morning.

We began looking forward to Sundays when, after Mass, we'd head over to Todt Hill for dinner. Disappointed that she didn't get us for the whole weekend, Grandma Jennie would stuff a weekend's worth of food into that one afternoon. In between courses my father and his parents strategized about the custody situation. His partner in the medical practice, Steve Fishman, MD, had referred him to his father, an attorney on Long Island. The elder Mr. Fishman said that in family court the only real consideration was the best interest of the child, and that presumption favored the mother. That meant the only way our father was getting custody was if he proved Mom was unfit, and dirty fingernails weren't going to cut it.

In the legal sense, "unfit" meant she neglected us or exposed us to some harm or danger. Proving this would be exceedingly difficult. Mom did not have a drug or alcohol dependence problem. She was also well educated, holding a master's in biology. She was active in my Cub Scout troop and the PTA, and we were all excelling in school. We were, for the most part, well-adjusted kids with one small problem: our parents hated one another with a passion.

When Mr. Fishman did not paint an optimistic picture, our father went to another attorney, Paul LeMole. Although LeMole specialized in criminal defense, his name carried a lot of weight in the Staten Island courts. His influence didn't cross the Verrazano Bridge, however, and he advised my father that if the custody case took place in Brooklyn, he wouldn't have a shot.

LeMole agreed with Fishman on one point: the chances of our father getting custody of all three of us were slim to none. Instead he should try to pick us off one at a time, starting with the oldest. If he got custody of me, LeMole believed, Stephen and Kevin would eventually follow. Our father liked what he was hearing. Compliments of Grandma Jennie, our father gave LeMole his retainer, and LeMole gave him some preliminary instructions. They were still going to try to paint Mom as an unfit mother. Even if they couldn't, with the right judge and testimony Dad could still win custody because they were only going after me.

With that my father put his plan into action. It began by taking all three of us to psychiatrists.

"If Mommy lived on one side of the block," the first shrink asked, "and Daddy lived on the other, where would you want to live?"

"The middle," I replied, and it was the truth. I loved certain aspects of life in Canarsie and other aspects of life in Staten Island. Obviously this wasn't enough for my father to build his case, so when we went to the next psychiatrist, he instructed me to say that living with my mother was very stressful for me. Specifically I was to say I'd seen Mom and David Karmi in bed naked together and was having nightmares as a result.

Until then my brothers and I had been a package deal, inseparable and thick as thieves. Now, however, my father and LeMole sought to drive a wedge between my mother and me, and if my relationships with Kevin and Stephen were casualties, so be it. While I wanted to please my father more than anything, I was nervous about leaving my mom and brothers. I had stayed in Staten Island without them only once. On one of our weekend visits, I had contracted a bad case of poison ivy, and since my father was a doctor and Rita was a nurse, Mom agreed to let me stay there for treatment. Despite the fact that I was itchy and miserable, my father took the opportunity to speak to me alone. He had a plan, and he didn't want Stephen or Kevin to know because he was afraid they'd say something to Mom.

As I lay in bed trying desperately not to scratch, my father sat on the edge, a new first-baseman's mitt in his huge left hand and a bottle of oil in the right. As Rita applied a foul-smelling pink lotion to my rash, he applied oil to the glove. As he rubbed he explained the plan he had cooked up. One day I would slip out of Mom's and into the alley behind the house. Grandpa Frank would be waiting around the corner on

Paerdegat Fourteenth Street, and he'd drive me to the other side of Seaview Park, where my father would be waiting; then the three of us would drive back to Staten Island. The key part of the plan was that I then had to tell everyone I had taken a taxicab to Staten Island completely of my own volition. My father couldn't stress the importance of this enough. If people found out that he had picked me up, he would go to jail. The plan would be implemented over the summer, after we had stayed with my father and Rita for the month of July.

Unaware of my father's plan to kidnap me, Mom had agreed to the long visit, and my brothers and I couldn't wait. While it was modest compared to the houses he would later build, the Grasmere house was kid-friendly, with a basketball hoop and a nice-size yard. It was also stocked with enough junk food to double as a Hostess outlet. That month our father pulled out all the stops. He took us to a Mets doubleheader, and, unlike David Karmi, he cursed both the Mets and the umpires when they lost both games. He also bought us a home plate and bases so we could play at the house. In the finished basement there were air hockey and ping-pong tables as well as a tremendous electric train set that had been my father's when he was a kid. Also brought over from Shangri-La were all our toys from Christmases past. With so much to do, it never even crossed our minds to play Mean Joe Green or our other Brooklyn games.

But, as much fun as it was, I started to miss Canarsie. My best friend on the block, David Herlands, even called me to find out what day I was getting home. Wednesday, I told him, hoping my father had forgotten about the plan. He hadn't. That morning he got me up before Stephen and Kevin, and we went outside. He had the baseball mitt in his hand again, but this time he tossed a ball into it as he went over the details. That afternoon, when he dropped us off, I was to sneak through the alleyway behind the house. I would find Grandpa Frank waiting in his Pontiac near the second dip on Paerdegat Fourteenth Street.

Nervous, I asked Dad if we could postpone it for two weeks. Herlands had told me we were going to have a block party over the weekend, and I didn't want to miss it. My father was forcing me to make a decision that would forever change my life and the lives of many others, and I wanted to postpone it for a block party. Still this was probably the most normal thought I had that whole day. I was only nine years old, and although I didn't understand all the ramifications of the plan, I was under a tremendous amount of pressure. Today, when I see how young and carefree most nine-year-olds are, I think, *No wonder I'm nuts.* How could a child that age have handled such a choice? Looking back I realize the choice was never really mine, and my request for more time fell on deaf ears because my father insisted it had to be done that day.

When he dropped us off in Canarsie that afternoon, Mom was ecstatic to see us. After showering us with hugs and kisses, she gently informed us that she had some bad news. All six of our toads from the Frog Tree had died. Mom had allowed us to keep the toads in white buckets on the wrought-iron balcony upstairs. She had promised to feed them while we were away, and she did. Then Fourth of July weekend came, and she went away to escape the city heat. It turned out to be one of the hottest on record in New York City, and when she returned she found two toads missing and four dead. They hadn't just died either; they had been cooked alive. The wrought iron had gotten so hot the toads melted to the bottom of the bucket. It was an awful sight. Mimi found the other two—they had jumped to their deaths and landed in the Vecchios' driveway.

To make it up to us, Mom had bought three water frogs that were now in a fish tank on the ledge in the kitchen. I was admiring them when the doorbell rang. It was David Herlands wanting to know if we wanted to come out to play running bases. I met him outside, half of me hoping I would get the opportunity to run to the alley, and the other half hoping I wouldn't. I didn't really want to go to Staten Island, but the thought of disappointing my father was unbearable.

When I heard the jingle of the ice cream truck a few minutes later, I knew this was my chance. David and the other kids ran toward the truck, reaching into their pockets for loose change, and I took off through the alley as my father had instructed.

When I got to Paerdegat Fourteenth Street, I looked around for Grandpa Frank. Finally I saw his car down the block parked next to the wrong dip. I ran over and got in, and we headed to meet my father by the park. He had me duck down when we crossed Remsen Avenue just in case Grandpa Jack was taking a walk around the neighborhood.

Within minutes of my disappearance, Stephen and Kevin went looking for me. They thought I had gone inside to see the frogs, but when they didn't see me, they went to get Mom. At first she wasn't worried; I had so many friends on the block, she figured I had gone into one of their houses. But as time went on, she started getting anxious. Neither she nor my brothers had any reason to suspect I was with my father, so when I didn't come home they started going to all my friends' houses. They even walked down to Paerdegat Ninth Street, where my friend Jeffrey Deutch lived. Of course no one had any clue where I was.

Mom didn't say anything to Stephen or Kevin, but she was starting to think I had been abducted by a stranger. She had always been petrified that one of us would be taken, and while I'm sure all parents have this fear, Mom's rose to the level of paranoia. Not only would she invoke ad nauseam the "don't talk to strangers" warning, but she would elaborate on what could happen to kids who didn't pay attention to their surroundings. There were a lot of men out there, she said, who like to touch little boys' penises. As if that weren't scary enough, she would tell us, "If a man ever tries to make you suck his penis, you run." In an effort to make us extra vigilant, she left little to the imagination. Kevin was especially frightened. Other than in school, he wouldn't go alone to a public restroom until he was a teenager.

In Mom's defense those were scary times in New York. The Son of Sam had been terrorizing the city, and everyone was on edge. Even the revenues at restaurants and nightclubs took a nosedive because people were afraid to leave their homes after dark. During the day my brothers and I would hang out with friends in the alleyway on the side of the Vecchios' house, talking about what we would do if the Son of Sam approached us. Emboldened by daylight and each other's company, we'd boast about pounding his head with a baseball bat then holding him down until the police came. But at night, alone in our beds, we were scared to death that we might be the .44-caliber killer's next victim.

When Mom and my brothers got back from Jeffrey Deutch's block, she called Aunt Paula in Wantagh, Long Island, and asked to speak with Uncle Jimmy, who was now a detective. He was at work, but Aunt Paula, hearing the hysteria in my mother's voice, said she would try to get a hold of him. Mom didn't dare call Grandma Dar, fearing she would scare her and Grandpa Jack to death.

At about eight-thirty that night, more than three hours after I'd left, Mom's phone rang. It was my father calling to say I was at his house and I had taken a taxicab to Staten Island because I wanted to live with him. At first Mom was just thankful I was alive. But when my father wouldn't even put me on the phone, she realized I had been kidnapped after all, just not by a stranger. She certainly didn't buy the ridiculous taxicab story, especially since just moments earlier I had been checking out the frogs and playing with my friends.

I had done it—I had carried out my father's plan without a hitch. I should have been thrilled, but on that first night it took me a long time to fall asleep. My head was spinning with a million thoughts. How could I live without my brothers? How long would it be before they moved to Staten Island? What would happen next? The only thing I was sure of was it felt good to make my father proud. In fact he'd done such a thorough job of brainwashing me against Mom that I hardly thought about her that night. When I did I wasn't thinking about how scared she must have been that afternoon or how she must have been crying because I chose to live with my father. Instead I lay in that bed thinking she would be mad that she'd no longer get my share of the child support.

A few days later, while my father was at work, the police came to the door. Rita didn't even answer. Instead the two of us hid in the hallway, listening as the doorbell and phone rang for what seemed like hours. The cops eventually left, but I wasn't allowed to leave the house for days. In the meantime my father had to go to the police station and get fingerprinted. He wasn't concerned. Interfering with custodial rights was a crime, but as long as I stuck to my taxicab story, they couldn't touch him. If I had gone of my own accord, it wasn't considered a kidnapping. Besides, these were the days before the enactment of the Parental Kidnapping Crime Act, and parents were rarely prosecuted for such abductions. As far as my father and the rest of the DeBlasis were concerned, possession was nine tenths of the law.

Paul LeMole was certainly earning Grandma Jennie's money. He managed to keep my father out of jail and the police from taking me back to Mom. He also outmaneuvered Mom's attorney, Herbert Berman, by petitioning for temporary custody before all the judges took off for August vacation. That aside, Herbert Berman was no slouch (he would go on to serve as a New York City councilmen for twenty-six years), and he told Mom this was only the beginning. As the mother she still had the upper hand. In the meantime, however, my father had scored a major victory, for it meant I would live with him and Rita throughout the proceedings, and he would be able to keep his grip on me.

It didn't take long for me to become bored with the electric train set in the basement. I also quickly realized the rest of the toys and games in the Grasmere house were useless without Stephen and Kevin. My half brother Frank was not quite a year and a half old, so asking him to tackle me in my green pajamas was out of the question. And I didn't even think about grabbing a knife and cutting through the floor. The house was a single-family ranch, so there was nothing to see below. Besides, it wouldn't be fun without Stephen and Kevin. I wondered what they were doing at home.

Now, instead of waiting for the weekend so I could go to Staten Island, I couldn't wait to see my brothers. Early on a Friday morning, my father stopped in my room before heading to work. Acting as if he had just found out, he told me that "the cunt from Canarsie" was not letting Stephen and Kevin come for the weekend. In fact, he said, his voice a perfect mix of sadness and indignation, it might be "a while" until we saw them.

While he was there, I ranted and raved about it being all my mother's fault, but as soon as my father walked out, I buried my face in my pillow, sobbing and sick to my stomach. Despite what I had said about Mom, I was really mad at Dad. I was sure he'd known all along that the other boys wouldn't be coming.

I didn't exactly know why he'd kept my hopes up; I just knew instinctively that he had.

Of course Mom was not going to let Stephen and Kevin come for the weekend! My father had just stolen her oldest son from her, and she certainly wouldn't give him the chance to get the other two. In fact she was so worried he would kidnap Stephen and Kevin, she and the boys spent the whole month of August away from Paerdegat Fifteenth Street. They alternated between Aunt Paula's house in Wantagh, Long Island, and Mom's friend Phyllis's house in Livingston, New Jersey. Even though they were safely out of Canarsie, they still weren't allowed to play out front.

Phyllis Wurzel was the kind neighbor who'd helped Mom out of so many tight spots after my father walked out. Her husband, Bernie, had also been a resident at Maimonides, and although the Wurzels eventually moved to Jersey, Phyllis and Mom had remained close.

Phyllis was a self-assured Jewish woman with short hair and an outgoing personality. My father couldn't stand her, and she wasn't a fan of his either. After the divorce their mutual disdain grew into mutual disgust. He called her "big-mouthed dyke Wurzel," and she referred to him as "Dr. Wonderful." She had been an elementary school teacher, but after having her daughter she retired and became a full-time mom. This left her plenty of time to visit Mom in Canarsie, and, as Bernie often worked late, she often stayed over at our house on Paerdegat Fifteenth Street. This prompted my father to accuse them of being lesbians, and he and LeMole debated whether I should tell the judge I had seen them lying in bed naked together. In the end they decided it was better if I just said I'd seen Mom in bed with David.

Once the police finally stopped coming around, my father let me play outside with Lenny and Stephen Zinanti, the two kids living next door. Just a month earlier, my brothers and I had practically ignored these kids. One day in July, they had been playing catch with their father when we'd pulled into the driveway. Lenny Zinanti had just thrown the ball as hard as he could. My father rolled his window down and shouted approvingly at Mr. Zinanti, "What an arm! What an arm!"

Mr. Zinanti smiled and waved, and my father turned to us and said, "He has an arm like a chicken." The three of us burst out laughing as our hero pulled the car into the garage. Now I was stuck playing with the butt of his joke. They weren't Stephen and Kevin, but playing with the Zinantis beat watching my father's electric train churn around the track for the zillionth time.

While I battled boredom through the month of August, my father reveled in his victory over my mother. As Labor Day approached, however, he realized he had a big problem: where to send me to school. According to LeMole he could get in more trouble for keeping me out of school than for abducting me. Although he had been granted temporary custody, LeMole advised my father that he couldn't pull me out of PS 115 in Canarsie. Legally Mom still had permanent custody and was the only one who could sign me out to another school. As a result I became one of the youngest commuters in the tristate area. For more than six months, my father shuffled me back and forth to PS 115. While it was only a twenty-mile drive, the Belt Parkway was—and still is—one of the deadliest stretches of bumper-to-bumper traffic on earth. Some days the commute would take two hours each way.

Still I was anxious to start the fifth grade and see my school friends. I had been away for only a month, but it had seemed a lot longer, and it was weird going back to Canarsie. On the first day of school, I was a mess. That morning my father had given me a twenty-dollar bill, telling me to hide it in my sock. It was emergency money, he said, to use on a cab in case Mom decided to kidnap me back. The whole thing was very confusing. I don't think my father would have expected or even wanted me to use the money for a cab back to Staten Island. I think the purpose of the twenty was to convince me, and anyone who might see the twenty, that I had paid for a cab to Staten Island in the first place. If that was the case, it worked. For a while I almost convinced *myself* that I had taken a taxi to his house over the summer.

On the ride to Brooklyn, my father would give me strict orders not to talk to Mom if she approached me. I didn't know what would happen if I saw her. I was looking forward to seeing Stephen and Kevin but wasn't sure if they were mad at me for leaving. When I finally did see Kevin in the hall, he ran away from me. The poor kid was even more confused than I was, probably because Mom had scared the shit out of him by saying my father might try to take him too.

One Friday I was in front of PS 115 waiting for my father,

who was running a few minutes late. Suddenly I saw my mother walking toward me. I stood there frozen, terrified she was going to start yelling or maybe even hit me. But as she got closer, I saw she was crying. Still she managed a smile as she bent down to hug and kiss me. I wanted to hug her back, but, remembering my father's orders, I stayed silent. If he pulled up and saw me with her, I'd never hear the end of it—how she only cared about the child support and that she'd put him in jail if anyone found out I hadn't taken the cab. If I had to pick the perfect moment to illustrate the control he had over me, that would be it. For all practical purposes, I hadn't seen my mother—a woman who had loved and taken care of me every day of my life—since the end of June. Yet all I could think of at that moment was my father's reaction if I disobeyed his order.

Luckily I didn't have to be afraid for very long. Mom quickly realized I was not allowed to talk to her and didn't force the issue. She just kissed me on the forehead, told me she loved me, and went inside to find my brothers. When my father came, I told him what had happened. He dismissed her tears as an attempt to make me feel bad, then changed the subject. But after that day, he was not only on time picking me up from school, but he often arrived twenty minutes early.

There was a lot of good stuff too. When my father was in a good mood, he never missed an opportunity to make me laugh. The last forty minutes of my school day was gym class. The teacher, Adolph Heiman, was a short, stocky older man who spit all over us when he spoke. He claimed to have invented a game he called Heiman Ball, which was basically dodge ball with a few extra rules. If anyone pointed that out, Heiman became incensed. "A monkey could play dodge ball, but it takes intelligence to play Heiman Ball!" It's really no wonder, given his name and megalomania, that the older kids started calling him Hitler.

I had told my father about my gym class, and since he was waiting for me to come out anyway, he decided to take a peek at the "nut," Mr. Heiman. The gym had a window so high up that anyone under six four wouldn't have been able to see inside. In fact if my father hadn't told me he was watching me, I never would have known. For months I was the only one who knew our gym class had a spectator. Then one day, during a game of Heiman Ball, Mr. Heiman noticed me mouthing something toward the window. When he saw the tuft of red hair, Heiman pulled me aside and asked me who the man was.

"My father," I said, shrugging, "He came from Staten Island."

Heiman blew his whistle, stopping all action in the gym. Pointing toward my father's hiding spot, he announced, "You see? I told you Heiman Ball was a great game. People come all the way from Staten Island to watch it!" My father and I laughed about that one the whole way home.

I got along with Rita too. After school she'd help me with my homework, then prepare a late dinner for us. When my father first suggested I call her Mom, I was reluctant. After a while he wore me down, but I still felt incredibly guilty whenever I said it. Still she was usually very kind to me, except for the one time when I saw—or heard—a completely different side of her. She was pregnant with my half brother, Matthew, at the time, but I never knew whether her rampage was because of morning sickness or genuine resentment.

I was lying in bed but had not fallen asleep yet when I heard screaming coming from the kitchen. It was Rita and my father having a rare but wicked fight.

"Every time I look at his face, I see Regina," Rita said. "I can't stand to look at him anymore. You should send him back!"

I quietly cried into my pillow the whole night, petrified that I would become an orphan. If Dad and Rita got rid of me, where would I go? There was no way Mom would take me back after I had left her like that. When I woke up the next morning, my eyes were so puffy I could hardly see. Rita was in the kitchen making my breakfast as if nothing had happened.

"Why are your eyes like that?" she asked.

"Don't know." I shrugged, afraid she would know I'd heard what she had said the night before. "I feel like I'm getting a cold."

That was the only time—at least that I'm aware—that Rita expressed any problem with my living there. After that night she resumed her role as my father's advocate; in fact whenever my father and I practiced my testimony for the various court hearings, Rita always sat in, offering her input on whether I should testify this way or that way. She certainly wasn't acting like someone who was sick of my face and wanted to send me back.

On the nights before we had court hearings, I'd be too

nervous to eat. When my father saw me lying on the floor, holding my side and complaining about the pains in my stomach, he would tell me I had nothing to be afraid of because he would be there with me. Then he'd joke that the whole custody situation was going to make me crazy when I was older. Laughing, he'd say that one day I would make all the newspapers for gunning people down with a rifle from a clock tower. He sure had a sick sense of humor; unfortunately, though he wasn't that far off with his predictions.

After eight months of brainwashing by my father, Rita, and to some extent LeMole, we were finally ready for court. From the beginning the chips were stacked in my father's favor. The case would be heard in Staten Island, and I had been sufficiently prepped to lie about my mother. These lies—essentially that Mom was openly sleeping with David Karmi—would be the heart of LeMole's case. Then there were the psychiatrists my father had taken me to see; they were to testify that after "extensive analysis" they had determined it was in my best interest to live with my father. At the tender age of ten, I was getting a crash course in American jurisprudence. Basically you pay someone a lot of money, and they'll tell the court whatever you want.

By the time a trial date was set, sometime in the spring of 1979, I had already met with the judge for a pretrial conference. I was nervous when LeMole and I entered his chambers, but the judge immediately tried to put me at ease. He asked me if I thought I was the smartest kid in my fifth-grade class. When I replied that there was a Chinese kid and a Jewish girl who might have been smarter, LeMole and the judge burst out laughing. The real joke was that it was the only truthful thing I'd say in the meeting. With flawless execution I went through my lines for the judge, telling him everything that was supposedly going on between Mom and David. After years of having it pounded into my head, I was finally going to tell the judge, "I want to live with my father."

As it turned out, however, it would be my only performance. Mom, seeing the futility of the situation, decided to give up the fight. Looking back it's not that surprising. Even before my alleged taxi ride to Staten Island, I had become my father's puppet, complaining about how Mom mismanaged the money he gave her for child support. Back then I had been spending only every other weekend with him, Mom reasoned, so what would I be like after living with him full time? In March 1979, with her capitulatory consent, my father gained permanent custody of me. Just like that the case we had been fixated on for months was over. No shots had been fired, but there would be plenty of casualties.

The DeBlasis celebrated with a feast at Grandma Jennie's, where the whole family oohed and ahhed over me, saying how proud they were of their "little man." Only Uncle Mike and Aunt Kathy lacked enthusiasm. Uncle Mike had been close with Mom before the divorce and knew she had gotten a raw deal. And, having been a psychology major in college, he also knew that nothing good could come from separating a child from his mother and siblings. But who was he to say anything to Grandma Jennie and her Joseph? They had never paid any attention to him before, and they were certainly not going to start now.

Mike and Kathy never said anything to me either, but it was pretty obvious how they felt. My cousin Frank was always asking, "Don't you miss your mother?"—no doubt repeating sentiments he had heard at home.

"Did you really take a cab from Brooklyn?" he asked one day as we played in Grandma Jennie's driveway. I glanced over at Grandpa Frank's Pontiac, dying to tell him, "Yeah, its license plate was...." But I didn't. Even though the case was over, my father held me to my vow of silence about how I had gotten to Staten Island that day. I didn't like lying to everyone about the taxi or about Mom, but whenever my father spoke about how we were "sticking together," I'd shove those thoughts aside and bask in the glow of his praise. Even with my half brother Frank around and Matthew on the way, there was no doubt my performance before the family court judge had solidified my position as the apple of my father's eye.

There was only one issue left to settle, and that was the court-mandated visitation with Mom. Court or no court, my father did not want me spending weekends with her; in fact if he had it his way, she wouldn't see me at all. But he wasn't going to fight it because Mom still had one rather large bargaining chip: my brothers. If he did anything to jeopardize her visitation with me, he would never see Kevin and Stephen and never get the opportunity to steal them away from her as well. Still he insisted that she see me only every other Saturday. In return Mom got the court to reduce his visitation with Stephen and Kevin to every other Sunday.

Prior to the first visitation, the court mandated a family counseling session with a psychiatrist. In attendance were Mom, Dad, Rita, Stephen, Kevin, and me. I don't remember what was said. All I can remember is that having all of us in the same room together was too much for Kevin. As soon as the session started, my seven-year-old brother retreated under a desk and pretended to be a dog for the entire hour. He would not come out until everyone but Steve left the room. I can still hear his fake bark.

When the visitation order finally took effect, I was both excited and terrified. While I desperately wanted to see Stephen and Kevin, I dreaded facing my mother, especially after snubbing her outside PS 115. I didn't know whether she'd be mad at me or try to talk me into coming back to live with her; I also didn't know what would be worse. It was like there were two Josephs, one living on Staten Island with my father and the other lingering in Canarsie with Mom, Kevin, and Stephen.

On the morning of my first visit with Mom, I awoke with my stomach in knots. At least she was taking us to the Statue of Liberty, so we wouldn't be sitting around the apartment looking for something to say to each other. Aunt Paula was coming too, and I was grateful for the extra buffer.

As it turned out, my fears were unfounded. Things were awkward between my brothers and me for about five minutes, then it was as if no time had passed. My mother didn't say one thing about moving back; in fact she was painfully nice. Still, after all my father's brainwashing, she felt like a stranger to me, and our conversation was stilted and formal. All day I was quiet and polite and felt completely isolated from them. I don't think I heard a word the tour guide said because I was so busy counting the hours until I could return to Dad and Rita.

A few weeks later, Mom took Stephen, Kevin, and me to lunch at a diner on Staten Island. This visit was even worse than the Statue of Liberty trip because this time, Phyllis Wurzel tagged along, and she didn't shut up for a minute. "What's it like living with your father?" "How is it having a strange woman acting like your mother?" "Do they make you change baby diapers?" I responded with grunts and shrugs, hoping she would get the hint. But the questions kept coming and coming. It was like sitting across the table from a pit bull, and I left the diner with the burger and fries still on my plate and my stomach growling.

As soon as I walked in the door, my father wanted to know about the lunch. When I told him about Phyllis, he went ballistic. Within minutes he was dialing the number of Bernie Wurzel's New Jersey office.

"You tell that big-mouthed, dyke cunt wife of yours to mind her own fucking business," he screamed as soon as Bernie answered. "If she opens her mouth to Joe again, I'll kill the two of you."

My father slammed down the phone and turned to me, his face beet red from the exertion, and said, "Bernie must have shit in his pants."

Poor Bernie. He hadn't even known that Phyllis had been

on Staten Island, let alone that she had talked to me. As out-going and aggressive as Phyllis was, Bernie was the opposite. He was shy and reserved and always minded his own business. Phyllis never said another word to me. In fact it would be years before I saw her again.

CHAPTER 7

Oedipus No More

As soon as my father got permanent custody, he wasted no time in pulling me out of PS 115 and enrolling me in St. Joseph's Catholic School on Staten Island. It was good-bye Heiman Ball and hello school uniforms, and after a few months of religious instruction and Dad's very generous donation to the parish, I received Confirmation with the rest of the fifth graders. I had received my Holy Communion just a few weeks earlier with a very proud Grandpa Frank serving as godfather. All in all I was acclimating easily to my new life; even the therapist the court had ordered me to see following the change in custody couldn't quite believe it. I was getting straight A's and making friends at St. Joseph's, and I was a rising star on my Staten Island Little League team. Most importantly I was showing no signs of wanting to climb a clock tower with a rifle.

Just as public schools weren't good enough for a doctor's son, neither was a modest three-bedroom ranch in Grasmere. My father was moving us back to Todt Hill, only this time to a huge five-bedroom house he was building one block from the country club where he and Rita had been married. The only problem was this would cost a small fortune that he didn't have. He'd have to sell the Grasmere house before beginning construction, which meant we'd have no place to live until the new house was finished. Of course he looked to Grandma Jennie to put us up for a few months. He also looked to her for the additional $10,000 the bank required for escrow. Not surprisingly she said yes to both requests without blinking an eye.

She may not have been able to say no to her Joseph, but neither was she standing at the door with arms open wide. This time it wasn't just Dad and one of her beloved grand-sons looking for a place to stay; he was bringing Rita, who Grandma Jennie still wasn't crazy about, and two babies. Besides, Grandma Jennie already had her hands full: Great-Grandma Termini had just died, and taking care of Pop, who was in his mid-nineties and senile, was a 24-7 job. The family had suggested putting him in a nursing home, but Grandma Jennie wouldn't hear of it. One time my father and the MRT had signed him into a home behind her back. When she found out, all hell broke loose. Pop was home that night, and there was no more talk of nursing homes. Grandma Jennie hired a Jamaican nurse named Gloria to help, but she still took a very hands-on role in Pop's care.

As if that weren't enough, Grandma Jennie was still working for the Internal Revenue Service as a chief auditor. Each morning she took the express bus from Staten Island to their lower Manhattan office, where she sifted through the tax returns of the rich and famous, including the Kennedys. If someone—no matter who they were—handed her a return or receipt that looked fishy, she'd look them straight in the eye and say, "You don't want to give me this" before handing it back to them. Her reputation was such that when accountants found out she was in charge of an audit, they'd instruct their client to bring a large check. Some cagey CPAs would try to reschedule in the hope that another auditor would be assigned on the new date. She knew all their tricks, and nothing got by her. Instead of wasting her talents on greedy taxpayers, Uncle Sam should have sent her to Vietnam. If they had, Saigon never would have fallen to the Vietcong. Grandma Jennie was that tough.

She loved her job, claiming it was relaxing compared to the rigors of housework. In her twenty-five years at the IRS, she did not call in sick once, which might explain why she had no patience for the younger girls at the office. Whenever one of them sighed and said they needed a break, Grandma Jennie rolled her eyes and snapped, "You just took a break. Get back to work." But she wasn't expecting anything of them that she didn't expect of herself. Each morning she was up at 5:00, and she made sure Grandpa Frank was up too so she could make their king-size bed. After a light breakfast of jellied toast and coffee, she'd head to the office and work right through lunch. Maybe she was saving room for whatever delicious meal her mother had waiting when she got home. Now that Great-Grandma Termini had passed away, Grandma Jennie had to cook every night in addition to cleaning and caring for her ailing father.

With our moving in, she'd have another five people to wait on. Grandma Jennie had always loved taking care of her family; however, that didn't include letting her new daughter-in-law sit on her ass all day watching soaps. Rita was laboring under the impression that since she had two infants to care for, she didn't have to help around the house. She didn't offer to cook or clean, and, according to Grandma Jennie, she "had her crap laid out all over the place." There were boxes, cribs, and playpens in the living room, baby toys in the kitchen, and mounds of clothes piled on the MRT'S old sofa bed. The mess was driving my fastidious grandmother crazy.

Worse still, she and my father appeared in no hurry to leave. Rita—or Her Highness, as Grandma Jennie called her—did not want to move into the new house until everything down to the last piece of crown molding was perfect. Whereas most women would have jumped at the chance to move into a spacious new house that just needed some finishing touches, Rita was content living out of boxes in Grandma Jennie's living room. We were only supposed to be there for a few months, yet six months later we were still there.

I couldn't have been happier about our extended stay; after all it was the great times in this house that had made me want to live with my father in the first place. Grandpa Frank and I played cards and watched *Hogan's Heroes* together, and Grandma Jennie was always in the kitchen making her delicious food. They both came to all my school and sports events. I made friends with the Esposito kids next door, whose backyard was so big it had a baseball diamond. Even without Kevin, Stephen, and the MRT living there, life was almost as good as it had been during the Shangri-La days.

Rita, however, was about to find out what every accountant in lower Manhattan already knew: you don't fuck with Vincenzina Termini DeBlasi. One Saturday night our babysitter, Rose O'Rourke, came by the house. Shortly after I had moved to Staten Island, Mrs. O'Rourke, whose grandson Tommy was my classmate at St. Joseph's, had started watching my half brothers and me when my father and Rita went out. This routine had continued while we were staying at Grandma Jennie's.

That night, when Mrs. O'Rourke walked into the house, Grandma Jennie was there to greet her. "Excuse the mess," she said just loud enough for Rita and my father to hear. "I normally don't live like this.... My son and daughter-in-law don't seem to mind it."

Dad and Rita left without saying anything, but later that night, after I had gone to bed and Mrs. O'Rourke had gone home, I was startled awake by the sound of my father's screaming. I sat straight up, not sure at first what he was saying or who he was saying it to.

"How dare you insult my wife?" he roared, "You never liked her from the start. You disrespect her. You disrespect me."

With the exception of my mother, I had never heard him yell at anyone like that. And at *Grandma Jennie*? I was shocked.

My grandmother gave as good as she got. "You treat this house like it's a shit hole! We never liked her? She never gave us a chance to like her. She is a lazy ingrate."

Even Grandpa Frank got in on the action, calling Rita "a coalminer's daughter" and a "secondhand piece of shit."

The battle royale continued late into the wee hours, and the following day we moved out.

"Now you're not going to see your grandchildren," Dad snarled as he walked out the door.

Already upset by the fight and our sudden departure, I nearly burst into tears when he wouldn't even let them kiss me good-bye. The past six months had been among the best of my life; now not only did I rarely see my mother, brothers, and Paladino grandparents, but I had lost Grandpa Frank and Grandma Jennie as well.

Although the new house was less than a mile from Grandma Jennie's, it might as well have been a continent away. The rift that had started over a messy house was growing deeper with each passing day, and I began to think I would never see my grandparents again. The only one not upset about the situation was Rita. With the new house ready, she and Dad didn't need Grandma Jennie anymore, and this fight presented the perfect opportunity to cut the apron strings once and for all.

Grandma Jennie wasn't about to apologize either, and my father knew it. He also knew he could use his kids to punish her, and, just as he had once instructed me not to talk to my mother, he now gave the same orders regarding Grandma Jennie and Grandpa Frank. Weeks then months went by without seeing or hearing from them.

Even as he was isolating his parents, my father was stepping up his efforts to get all of his sons under one roof. Until then he hadn't pushed Kevin and Stephen to come live with us because he couldn't afford another custody case while he was building the house. Now that we had moved in and his younger sons were out of diapers, he recommitted himself to getting my brothers.

Kevin would be the tougher sell; he was the baby and especially close to Mom. So my father started with Stephen. Knowing Stephen was a little jealous of the attention Mom gave Kevin, he played his middle son like a piano. He told him a series of "truths" that would occur if he stayed in Canarsie:

"If you stay in Canarsie…you'll always play second fiddle to Kevin."

"If you stay in Canarsie…you'll go to junior high and high school with a bunch of *shvatzas*. Is that what you want?"

"If you stay in Canarsie…." It went on and on, and it was as powerful a campaign as when he banged his big freckled fist on the table and shouted, "Tell the judge…."

Never opposed to putting me in the middle of his battles, he now enlisted me to help with Stephen's recruitment. I knew Stephen liked Rita's tuna-fish sandwiches, so I told him, "If you come live with us you can eat tuna sandwiches every day."

But it wasn't the tuna sandwiches or the fear of the shvatzas that swayed Stephen. Ever since he was a little kid, Stephen had wanted to live in a mansion. To this day Grandma Dar says, "When Stevie was little, he always talked about being rich and living in a big house with a pool and a tennis court."

Now he had his chance. By the time my father and I started

bribing him, he was already complaining to Mom that they couldn't afford Jordache jeans and Adidas sneakers. And by June 1981, Stephen had made up his mind: he wanted to live in a mansion and eat tuna poolside.

Stephen's change of residence was much less dramatic than mine. There were no phantom taxicab rides, bitter fights, or high-priced attorneys. With a little coaxing from Dad, Stephen confided to a psychiatrist he was depressed over Mom's giving all her attention to Kevin. He poured it on thick too, telling the shrink he'd even thought about killing himself. When the psychiatrist told Mom, she simply agreed to let Stephen live with us. There was never even a legal change of custody. Over the years she had learned that it was futile to fight my father; after all she had lost so much to him already. Maybe this way, she thought, he'd leave Kevin alone.

On July 8, 1981, Stephen moved into the Todt Hill house. I remember the date because it was also Kevin's tenth birthday. Kevin came to Staten Island that day, and while he was there he received his presents from my father: a new baseball glove and the news that for the second time in three years, an older brother would be moving away from him. Devastated, Kevin cried the whole car ride back to Canarsie. Dad tried to cheer him up by speeding over the dips on Paerdegat Fourteenth Street, but Kevin only cried louder with each bump. This wasn't one of those post-divorce magical visits to Shangri-La; Kevin's world was falling apart. I could relate. It was the same way I had felt when I'd found myself brother-less back in 1978. The only difference was I had been afraid to show emotions to my father—or to my mother for that matter.

There was no celebratory dinner by Grandma Jennie's house for Stephen's arrival. Dad and Grandma Jennie were still at war, and we had not seen her in over a year. Mom, who had always joked that our father had an Oedipus complex, couldn't believe it when Kevin told her about the rift. Unfortunately for her Kevin had no idea why Dad and Grandma Jennie weren't speaking, and whenever he asked me I just told him they'd had an argument. Dying to know what it had been about, she told Kevin she'd give him a hundred dollars if he uncovered the whole story.

If Mom was shocked that Oedipus wasn't speaking with his mother, she was stunned speechless when one day in August 1981 she picked up the phone and heard Grandma Jennie on the other end. The last time Grandma Jennie had spoken with a Paladino was when Grandma Dar told her to flush her head down the toilet in 1972. After the way the DeBlasis—including Grandma Jennie—had treated Mom after the divorce, she had every right to slam down the phone, but that wasn't her style. Besides, this was her chance to find out what had happened between Grandma Jennie and my father.

To my mother's disappointment, Grandma Jennie didn't go into the details of the fight; she just said she and her son had "a falling out," and he wasn't letting her see her grandchildren. She was calling to ask if Kevin could stay with her for the week. Mom agreed, but it wasn't because she felt bad for Grandma Jennie. There was absolutely no love lost there, at least on Mom's end. For her part Grandma Jennie was probably wishing Mom was still her daughter-in-law instead of the coalminer's daughter.

Ironically, Mom allowed the visit for the same reason Rita and Grandma Jennie had teamed up during my custody battle: an enemy of an enemy is a friend. As much as Mom hated Grandma Jennie, she hated my father more. She knew he was using us to punish his mother, and she took the opportunity to stick it to him by letting Kevin go. His reaction when he learned that Grandma Jennie had called and asked her permission.... Well, that would be icing on the cake.

Mom was right. Kevin had been at Grandma Jennie's house for about five days when the MRT's wife, my aunt Carolyn, opened her big mouth. "It's so nice," she told Rita, "that Regina let Kevin stay at Jennie's for the week."

As soon as he found out Kevin was on Todt Hill, my father flew over to Grandma Jennie's and demanded she hand him over.

"Over my dead body," Grandma Jennie told him, much in the same tone that she used to boss around the tax attorneys and CPAs at work. "He's not going anywhere. His mother has custody of him, and she wants him here for the week."

As big, loud, and intimidating as my father is, he had nothing on Grandma Jennie. Not only did Kevin end up staying the week, but a few weeks later Rita and Dad finally apologized to Grandma Jennie. While Grandma Jennie quickly resumed hosting dinners and attending our school and sports competitions, things were never the same. The dirty laundry had been aired, and harsh words, once spoken, are impossible to take back.

CHAPTER 8

Stevie, Stevie, Stevie

Shortly after the reconciliation, Grandma Jennie attended Stephen's school play at St. Joseph's. She couldn't believe that although he had been at the school for only a little over a month, everybody knew him, especially the girls. According to my grandmother, hoards of females were screaming, "Stevie, Stevie, Stevie" throughout the performance. She also told people, "My handsome grandson, Joseph, was at the school three years and no girls ever cheered for him."

Stephen had taken the school by storm, quickly becoming the most popular kid in the sixth grade—maybe even the whole school. It wasn't like I had taken him around and showed him the ropes either. In fact I pretty much ignored him for the first week. I had been embarrassed that a brother of mine just appeared out of nowhere, especially since I had never even mentioned to any of my friends that my parents were divorced or that I had brothers in Canarsie.

I got over the embarrassment in a hurry. Kids were coming up to me in the hall and asking, "Why didn't you tell me you have such a cool brother?" Boys and girls alike were drawn to Stephen. He seemed always to wear the right clothes and have the right hairstyle. It didn't hurt that he was also a terrific athlete who excelled in whatever sport he picked up.

Stephen was also a favorite around the house. Unlike me he was very neat and organized. He kept his closet in order and always made his bed. He was also much more attentive to our half brothers, Frank and Matthew, than I was. While he was happy to play with them all day, I always grew bored after a few minutes. He would even wipe their asses—literally, since Rita put him in charge of taking them to the bathroom. Those kids adored Stephen. They would sleep on the floor next to his bed just to be around him.

Stephen also won points for being helpful in the kitchen. He had been that way ever since we were little. Mom liked to sleep in on the weekends, and we got up early and ravenously hungry. Stephen put himself in charge of making breakfast, and what he lacked in skill he made up for in resourcefulness. If we were out of milk, he'd pour juice onto our cereal, lisping, "Juith is good too, ya know." One time he even tried making us French toast, but Mom took over after she awoke to the smell of burning butter.

He had always tried to help Grandma Jennie too, even sneaking out of bed at 4:00 a.m. to watch her bread chicken cutlets or fry meatballs for the next day's feast. By age eleven Stephen had enough experience to become an excellent housewife.

Other kids in my situation might have been jealous of Stephen. I had helped convince him to live with me only to have him outshine me in sports as well as in popularity at school and at home. But I had no hard feelings. In fact, as a generally lazy person, I was happy to have him around. Every time he wiped Matthew's ass or skimmed the pool, it let me off the hook from having to do those disgusting chores. I didn't resent his popularity with the girls at school either. Besides, as it turned out, I would soon have my hands full at home.

CHAPTER 9

Starting to Blow

For as long as I had known Rita, she had liked to blow-dry my hair after I washed it. She had done the same with Stephen and Kevin going back to when we all visited Grasmere and she was making the claim that Mom didn't bathe us properly. She'd wash our hair in the sink, then, after drying it, she'd ask for a thank-you kiss on the cheek. Even after I had outgrown the sink and moved to the shower, Rita still dried my hair. Slowly the thank-you kisses moved from her cheek to her lips. Then, just as gradually, the lips began to part, and our tongues would touch. When the adult kisses started in the bathroom, it didn't seem all that strange. Besides, it always happened so fast, and the next thing I knew one brother or another would be coming into the bathroom to shower.

By the time I was thirteen, I was getting too old for her to blow-dry my hair; however, I hadn't outgrown getting tucked in at night. After putting Frank and Matthew to sleep, Rita would come in to give me a good-night kiss. These good-night kisses were longer and more passionate than the thank-you kisses, and my pubescent body certainly took notice. My mind, however, was completely confused. Getting your first real hard-on is weird enough, let alone when you get it from French kissing your stepmother in your bed with your father a few doors down. By that time I knew it wasn't normal, but I didn't care. It felt too good. I began routinely having wet dreams, but I still had no clue what masturbation was. In fact I didn't begin beating off until college. But, as my brother Kevin says, "You didn't need to. You had Rita."

Around that time the whole family went to Rita's hometown, Old Forge, Pennsylvania, to visit her dying father. Amerigo Sylvani had been a handsome man. He had also been a coalminer and a heavy smoker, which meant he was practically begging for the lung cancer that would eventually spread to his brain and kill him. Amerigo's wife, Oliria, was a warm, rather plain-looking lady. They were both on the short side, which was odd considering Rita and her younger brother Marco were taller than average.

I was dreading the trip and not just because of Amerigo's illness. Old Forge was the most boring place on earth. Dad took us there every summer, and we'd spend the week hanging around the cramped, rundown house waiting for Amerigo to emerge from his wine cellar piss drunk. He'd spout his Chianti-fueled wisdom until Rita and Oliria could coax him into bed. It was the only excitement around.

Outside was a huge vegetable garden where a black cloud of horseflies entertained themselves by swarming around the large piles of dung that were scattered among the rows of tomatoes and zucchini. The dung was courtesy of Shirant, Rita's dog. At least I think she was a dog. Shirant was so large, she could have passed for a small pony. One summer when Kevin was about six, Shirant's leash, a long, interlocking metal chain, got twisted around his legs. Shirant was barking and panting, and Kevin was screaming. My father rushed over and freed him, but the damage had been done. To this day he is still afraid of dogs big and small.

Shirant didn't endear herself to Grandma Jennie either. One summer before the blowup on Todt Hill, she and Grandpa Frank were invited to Old Forge to celebrate Rita's grandmother's eightieth birthday. Unimpressed by the house, they stayed in a hotel but came to the Sylvanis' for dinner. One night, right before the meal, Grandma Jennie witnessed Shirant eating her own feces. Grandma Jennie was so sick, she couldn't touch her dinner. The evening was topped off by one of Amerigo's drunken performances. That was Grandma Jennie's last time in Old Forge. I can only imagine her conversation with Grandpa Frank on the long car ride back to Staten Island as they lamented the days when they celebrated birthdays with the Paladinos. Grandpa Jack never got drunk, and Grandma Dar didn't allow pets in their immaculate house.

Normally we stayed with the Sylvanis, but when Rita's father was dying, Dad sprung for a motel—one room for six people. Dad took one look at the two double-size beds and decided it would be best to split up the two adults. Rita, Frank, and I shared one bed while Dad, Stephen, and Matthew slept in the other. I spent that first night with my hand nestled between Rita's ass cheeks. I slept maybe twenty minutes, and by morning my underwear was saturated. A few feet away my father slept with Stephen's feet and Matthew's dirty diaper mere inches from his face.

Amerigo died two weeks later. Unfortunately, when we went back for the funeral, we stayed at the house.

CHAPTER 10

Meet the Beave

By the time I was fourteen, I had been to two weddings—when my father married Rita at the country club on Todt Hill and when the MRT finally got off Grandma Jennie's sofa bed to wed Aunt Carolyn. Each affair had been a blast with plenty of cousins to hang out with, surf-n-turf, and a Venetian hour that rivaled the dessert spreads at Grandma Jennie's holiday parties.

But when I received a third wedding invitation, I didn't want to go. Mom was getting remarried. Relatives I hadn't seen since moving to Staten Island in 1978 would be there, not to mention Phyllis Wurzel and her big mouth. But that wasn't the only reason I dreaded going. I hadn't seen my mother in over a year and a half. After Stephen moved to Staten Island, neither of us visited her that often. She didn't really force the issue because Kevin wasn't visiting us in Staten Island either. She had become increasingly uneasy about letting him go, fearing—with good reason—that he wouldn't come back. The visits in both directions had become less and less frequent until they finally stopped altogether.

This time I couldn't count on my father's animosity toward Mom to save me from going. He was thrilled she was getting married because it meant he would no longer be responsible for alimony or rent. Stephen and I figured he wanted us to go just to make sure the wedding actually took place.

Even stranger was that Mom was marrying not longtime boyfriend David Karmi but a man I had never even met. She and David had been engaged for a while, but Mom called it off when she realized he'd forever be chasing the youth the Nazis had stolen from him forty years earlier. She'd already been married to one man who ran around on her, and she had no interest in a sequel. After she and David broke up, Mom dated a bit, but she didn't get serious with anyone until she met Steven "Beaver" Friedman at a singles party in Merrick, Long Island, on February 5, 1982. Beave, an American-born Russian Jew, was the same age as Mom and extremely good-looking. After meeting him Kevin told our father that Beave "looks like the guy who plays Superman but with big lips." The lips were all the more conspicuous because of their constant motion. Beave loved to talk, and he loved to eat.

While Mom had certainly traded up from my father in the looks department, Beave's finances were a different story. He was trying to support an ex-wife and two adopted children on an elementary schoolteacher's salary—no easy proposition— and supplemented his income by selling women's clothing at flea markets on weekends. Eventually he recruited Kevin as his helper. My youngest brother was only too happy to go. Abandoned first by his father then by his two older brothers, the poor kid was craving male camaraderie. He and Beave hit it off immediately.

Beave operated two vending booths behind the horse track at Roosevelt Field Raceway. To facilitate communication between them, he purchased two walkie-talkies and gave one to Kevin. Whenever Kevin had to radio Beave's booth, he'd say, "Ward to Beaver. Pick up, Beaver." He had started watching *Leave It to Beaver* reruns on TV and apparently thought he was bestowing a great compliment upon his future stepfather. In any event the name stuck, and to this day he's known to all of us not as Steve but as the Beave.

Just a few months after Beave and Mom began dating, he moved in with her and Kevin. They were still living on Paerdegat Fifteenth Street but not in Mr. Vecchio's house. In 1979 his job had transferred him to Costa Rica, and he took his family with him. Shortly thereafter Mom moved across the street to a bigger apartment in a row house built by David Karmi's construction company. So, in the months leading up to their wedding, Beave lived rent-free in an apartment paid for by my father and built by David Karmi. I don't know if it was Mom's way of snubbing both her exes, but her wedding to Beave—a Jewish ceremony performed by a rabbi—took place in that apartment one year to the day of their first meeting.

Stephen and I showed up two hours late to the wedding, missing the whole ceremony and a good part of the reception. The duplex was packed with friends and relatives; they filled every room and even lined the staircase, eating, laughing, and drinking. But the first person Stephen and I saw when we slipped up the stairs was Grandpa Jack. Almost eighty and wearing a yarmulke over his white hair, he looked less like the strapping man I remembered and more like the pope.

When our eyes locked, I felt like a deer caught in headlights. Although I had been close to Grandpa Jack and Grandma Dar before going to live with my father, I hadn't seen them since. What was worse I thought about them much less than I should have. My father had made it clear that anyone and anything connected to Mom was insignificant. My grandparents, who were overjoyed that their daughter was finally remarrying after eleven long years, tried to put me at ease. It didn't work. I spent much of the wedding making awkward small talk with them and other long-lost relatives, keeping tabs on Stephen in case I needed rescuing, and counting the minutes until Dad and Rita came to get us. It felt just like that first post-custody-battle visit with Mom at the Statue of Liberty: weird and uncomfortable, like half of me belonged and half of me didn't.

When Dad and Rita finally came, the first thing he asked was, "So, she actually went through with it, huh?" When Stephen and I said yes, he just smiled and nodded, thinking about the $500 he'd be saving each month. Then he turned back to us. "Did that cunt Wurzel say anything to you boys?"

While Dad was celebrating the end of his financial

obligation to my mother, my stolen moments with Rita were becoming more and more frequent. No longer satisfied with a good-night kiss, I had begun seeking her out during daylight hours in every room of Dad's fancy Todt Hill house. It was always the same: she'd resist at first (whether because she was playing a game or she felt genuinely scared or guilty, I don't know), then she'd start kissing me just as we did in my room at night. Normally we would kiss and grope until I ejaculated, which, since I was fourteen years old, didn't take too long.

Most of the time, other people were home, but the house was so big we weren't too afraid of getting caught. Of course if we heard someone coming, usually Frank or Matthew, we'd jump apart like two scalded cats. I lived for the rare occasion when Rita and I were home alone, but I had no problem approaching her even when my father was around. If he was downstairs and Rita was upstairs folding laundry, I would not hesitate to go up…and get off. One evening Rita and Dad were sitting across from each other at the kitchen table. Rita was typing an English paper for me. I pulled out the chair next to her, sat down, and, under the guise of reading the paper, leaned over and rested my hand on her upper thigh. It was sick.

Extra money must have been burning a hole in Dad's pocket, because before the paint dried on the Todt Hill house, he decided he wanted an even bigger one. He put an offer on a huge, gated mansion that overlooked the Verrazano Bridge. It was next door to the former home of Paul Castellano, the Gambino crime boss gunned down by John Gotti in front of a swanky Midtown steakhouse. I'm not sure which selling feature appealed to my father more, but it didn't matter because the deal fell through. Undeterred, Dad and Rita continued looking, first around Staten Island then expanding the search to New Jersey. Finally they decided on Holmdel, a rustic, upper-middle class community situated near the Jersey Shore and just an hour's drive from Manhattan. Dad found a huge plot of land on a hill overlooking a farm and began planning the biggest house Holmdel had ever seen.

Since he once again had to sell his current mansion before building the next, we had to find temporary accommodations and fast. Staying with Grandma Jennie wasn't even an option this time. She had put Shangri-La on the market about five minutes after she heard her Joseph was leaving Staten Island and taking her grandchildren with him.

Thus began the DeBlasi exodus to New Jersey. Grandma Jennie finally retired from the Internal Revenue Service and bought a brand-new house in Manalapan. Most people downsize when they stop working and sell the family home, but not Grandma Jennie; her new house was nearly twice as big as Shangri-La. Maybe she figured she needed that oversized garage for Grandpa Frank's 1978 Cadillac.

Uncle Mike and Aunt Kathy bought a house right across the street from her, and while Grandma Jennie was thrilled to have family around her, she was also sick of being the cash cow. When Uncle Mike asked her to help him with the closing costs, she told him to ask my father for the ten grand she had loaned him back in 1981. When Uncle Mike approached him, Dad insisted the money had been a gift. He then told his kid brother to get lost. Dad needed every last dollar to pour into his own palatial spread.

The people in gossipy Holmdel had to be wondering who Dad thought he was. There were businessmen in town with fifty times his net worth, yet they lived in houses half the size. The answer lay in Dad's showy Sicilian background. Building the biggest house in town was his way of telling these blue-bloods he had made it. While the house was being built, we moved into a rented four-bedroom ranch, and Stephen and I were enrolled in Holmdel High School.

Most kids would have been upset about having to start a new school, but not me. I had done my freshman year at Monsignor Farrell, a competitive, all-boys prep school on Staten Island. Most kids on Staten Island went to Catholic schools, but Jersey was different. Holmdel High was both public *and* coed, which sounded just fine to me and my brother.

My only gripe was with the rental house; it was much smaller than the Todt Hill house and only one floor, which threatened to put a crimp in my "load sessions" with Rita. But the added risk of exposure didn't stop me—or her for that matter—even after my half-brother Frank saw us. One day Rita and I were making out on the floor when we heard a high-pitched, "Are you two wrestling?" Seven-year-old Frank was staring down at us with a childish mixture of confusion and jealousy that he wasn't in on the game. We were more careful after that, but there had to be other occasions where he or Matthew saw us. Luckily they were too young to understand what they were seeing, and besides, as far as they knew, Rita was my and Stephen's biological mother. In fact they wouldn't learn the truth until after my first bout of mania in college.

My father certainly had no reason to suspect anything was going on between Rita and me. Even though I was a horny teenager, and Rita, in her early thirties, was quite attractive, she had known me since I was a young boy and had, for all intents and purposes, been my parent for several years. Not to mention the fact that Dad's mammoth ego would never allow him to suspect his wife of being unfaithful with anyone, let alone his own son.

He did worry, however, that Stephen and I would make the same mistake he had—namely marrying before we had time to sow our wild oats. To prevent this he forbade us from dating until the end of our senior year of high school. As a consolation prize, he ordered a few racy movie channels from the cable company, saying, "I don't want you guys walking around here with hot cocks." He sounded half serious, so maybe he *was* concerned about our being around his pretty, much younger wife. If so he certainly wasn't going to admit it outright.

On the other hand, he had no problem with us walking around the house in our underwear. He did too, and like ours, they weren't boxers but tighty-whities that left little to the imagination. We often wore nothing else as we sat around the dinner table, and I used to imagine a scandalized neighbor looking through the window and thinking we were a bunch of nudists. Only Rita wore clothes, even if it was just a nightgown or robe.

When we were *really* lucky, my dad, all three hundred

pounds of him, walked around the house in the nude. During my junior year, he took the whole family—including Kevin and Rita's mother, Oliria—to Disney World. Having his mother-in-law around did not deter Dad from walking around the hotel room in his drawers. "Joseph," Oliria snapped, "put some clothing on. You look disgusting."

The Florida climate must not have agreed with him, because while at Disney, Dad's hemorrhoids flared up along with a nasty cluster of cold sores around his mouth. The day we went to EPCOT, he confined himself to the hotel room. When we returned we found him lounging in bed, a surly expression on his face.

"How was EP-COCK?" he asked, smiling at his own joke, then he barely listened as Matthew recounted our day in painstaking detail.

When Frank asked him what he had done during the day, Dad snapped, "I tried to hit the screen from here. What do you think I did?"

I didn't know whether Frank or Matthew caught his meaning, but the rest of us did. He was saying he'd tried to see how far he could ejaculate. My father had always had a sick sense of humor and a way with words as well. Whenever my brothers and I did something he didn't approve of, he'd scream at me, "Do you have hair on your balls?" It was his crass way of saying that as the oldest, I should know better. This always elicited a glare and a "Joseph, don't be so disgusting" from Oliria.

Dad's ailments aside, it was a great trip, especially since Kevin was there. Stephen and I hadn't seen him since Mom's wedding nearly two years earlier. Around the time we moved into the rental house, he, Mom, and Beave had moved to Merrick, Long Island. Grandma Dar and Grandpa Jack, thrilled about their daughter's new start in life, gave them the down payment. Beave continued teaching, and Mom, who had gone back to school to become an X-ray technologist, took a job at Mercy Medical Center in nearby Rockville Centre. She soon found she hated taking X-rays, but with her master's in biology and prior teaching experience, she was soon hired as director of Mercy's School of Radiography. Years later I would be strangled by security guards at Mercy. So much for professional courtesy.

We had barely seen Kevin when he lived right over the bridge in Brooklyn; now that he was on Long Island, it was even less often. This was perfectly fine with Dad, who wanted everyone in Holmdel to think Rita was his first wife and we were the perfect family. For this charade to continue, however, Kevin could never be seen in Holmdel. After we moved there, Dad stopped trying to convince him to live with us, and Stephen and I were forbidden to tell anyone at school that Rita wasn't our real mother or that we had another brother. From then on we saw Kevin only when we took vacations away from Holmdel—usually once every year or two. By then this felt almost normal to me and probably to Stephen as well. It had to be difficult for Kevin, though, laughing and vacationing with his brothers one minute then the next getting dropped off in Merrick, an only child once more.

At the time I did not think it was strange that Dad went to

such lengths to keep his previous life—including his youngest son—a secret. Like everything else he said and did, I accepted it as law. Later on I realized he was simply carrying on a family tradition: just like Grandma Jennie never spoke of the fact that she had half siblings or that her father had been married before, Dad wanted everyone to think he had a traditional family. Rita was completely invested in appearances too; of course she had the added incentive of hiding her trysts with me.

My junior year at Holmdel High School began with a vicious bout of mononucleosis. I missed the first week of classes, and when I returned everyone teased me about who had given me the "kissing disease." *If you only knew,* I'd reply in my head.

One day I thought for a moment that they actually did know. Right before I got on the school bus that morning, Rita and I had one of our sessions. My underwear was still damp when I walked into homeroom. My best friend, Danny Chow, was already there, and as I walked toward my desk I heard him exclaim, "Motherfucker!" in my direction. For a split second, I thought somehow Chow, who was the smartest kid in the school, had figured out I was fooling around with my stepmom. Then I realized it was just a colorful greeting. I shrugged and smiled at the future valedictorian's lame attempt to appear cool, but my stomach was still flipping as I took my seat.

My relationship with Rita didn't stop me from noticing girls and even having crushes on a few of them. Holmdel High had its fair share of pretty ones, and just like on Staten Island, every one of them was in love with my brother, Stephen. Even as a freshman, he could have had his pick of any girl in school. The fact that he wasn't allowed to date—and therefore unattainable—only added to the allure.

While the same was true of me, I did not receive a fraction of the attention Stephen did. The giant pimple on the tip of my nose didn't help matters. This thing was the size of a gumball and lasted what seemed like the entire year. It was truly a character builder. The only girl who wasn't repulsed by it was Rita. I guess I had a face only a mother could love. Her attention certainly cushioned the blow of being the less popular DeBlasi brother at school.

By senior year, though, life had really begun to improve. I was voted as having the best physique in my class, and when I began the second semester Dad finally lifted the dating ban. Girls immediately showed interest, and soon I was seeing Suzanne Grubowski, the beautiful, green-eyed blonde who had been nominated for homecoming queen.

One night I took Suzanne to a house party in town. The date was uneventful until Suzanne, who was training to become an EMT, had to leave on an emergency call. She returned around twelve-thirty in need of food and a few minutes to unwind, so I took her to a diner and didn't get home until 1:30 a.m. The problem was Dad and Rita had set my curfew at midnight.

When I explained what had happened, my father was annoyed but didn't make a huge deal out of it. Rita, on the other hand, was livid. For the next hour, I sat in shocked silence as she ranted and raved about how I had defied her parental authority. You would have thought I had used the extra hour and a half to rob a bank; however, I began to suspect that my real crime was staying out late with the homecoming queen. As Rita played the role of the overprotective mother, I kept my face carefully neutral, afraid that Dad would somehow guess our secret. But inside I was thinking, *this woman is crazy*. My suspicions were confirmed during our makeup session the next morning, which was more passionate than ever, and I demonstrated to Rita that I hadn't forgotten about her.

Not everyone bought in to her concerned parent act as readily as my father did. Shortly after the incident with Suzanne, I went to another party, and this time Rita came to pick me up at midnight. By that hour the party was in full swing, and with all the noise I didn't hear the honking outside. At twelve-thirty I sauntered out of the house to find Grandma Jennie and Matthew sitting in the car with a crazed-looking Rita. Years later Grandma Jennie told me she couldn't believe how angry and upset Rita was getting in the car that night. It wasn't until Grandma Jennie found out about our incestuous relationship that she realized why her daughter-in-law was acting like such a lunatic.

There was only one time Rita actually fought me off. I had just gotten home from an early morning basketball practice. My father was already at work, and everyone else in the house, including Rita, was still in bed. Pumped and sweaty from the exercise, I walked into the bedroom she shared with my father and ripped the covers off her. She was lying there naked, all breasts and bush and milky-white skin. My eyes took it all in, including the Gorbachev-like beauty mark on her ass, which I had never seen before. Completely turned on, I jumped on top of her naked body, but Rita shoved me away long enough to pull the covers back over her. Apparently even she had her limits. No matter; I still got off, then I went downstairs and waited for her to make me French toast.

I wasn't all that surprised by her chilly response; after all nudity had never been part of our game. But, like any other teenage boy would have, I had taken a shot. That morning was the closest we ever came to sexual intercourse.

Later that day she drove me to the Department of Motor Vehicles. "You have nice tits," I told her in the car, not quite sure what her reaction would be. In the five years we had been fooling around, neither of us had ever said a word about it.

Rita was quiet for a minute, then I saw the blush spreading across her face. "Thanks."

Because we never spoke about it, I had no idea whether Rita felt guilty or not; there was certainly no evidence of inner turmoil as she allowed me to dry hump her in every corner of the house. For my part I didn't give the fact that we were betraying my father all that much thought. All I knew was that a hot older woman—who, despite what I called her, was not my real mom—wanted to fool around with me. Besides, I had essentially grown up this way; my make-out sessions with Rita were just another thing that went on in the house, like clearing the dinner table albeit much more pleasurable.

And it wasn't like I wasn't used to living a double life. Just like there was the Joseph who loved his mother but could be pressured to lie about her in court, there was also the Joseph who said and did everything to please his father yet still felt entitled to fondle Rita whenever he got the chance. Like every other aspect of my bifurcated life, I kept them completely separate from one another.

As high school drew to a close, however, I started thinking about how wrong it all was. Maybe it was because I was preparing to go off to college and start a new life, one that would not include daily romps with my stepmother. It would be over when I moved out, I thought, and instead of feeling disappointment or sadness, I felt only relief.

My first choice was the prestigious University of Pennsylvania. My father, who loved the idea of the apple of his eye going Ivy League, was ecstatic to learn that we had a connection to UPenn. Oliria's boss, Dr. Marmo of Old Forge had gone to the University of Pennsylvania Medical School. At my father's request, Dr. Marmo wrote a letter of recommendation for me; however, such letters, even from a distinguished alum, only go so far. My SAT score was only 1,100, and while I had shined at my Catholic school on Staten Island, my class rank at the more competitive Holmdel High was not up to Ivy League standards. When I got the rejection letter, I didn't know what was worse—that I wasn't going to UPenn or that I had disappointed my father.

I didn't dwell on it too long, though, because I had been accepted by Lehigh University, a top-ranked research school in Bethlehem, Pennsylvania. I was thrilled, but my father encouraged me to go to Rutgers instead. Rutgers, a state university, had been one of my safety schools, a last resort in case I didn't get in anywhere else. It was also much cheaper than the private and very expensive Lehigh. My father figured since I wouldn't graduate with an Ivy League pedigree, why should he pay Ivy League prices? Besides, he was up to his eyeballs in debt from the construction and upkeep of his Holmdel estate.

As usual I went along with his wishes. I would enroll at Rutgers in the fall. I was excited at the prospect of playing baseball there; the school had a good team, and I had always excelled at sports. The problem was I was too shy to call the coach to find out how one goes about trying out. So Dad, pretending to be me, called for the information. If only he had known that while I didn't have the balls to call the Rutgers baseball coach, I had been brushing my balls up against his wife all throughout junior high and high school. But my father wasn't the only one who was clueless. Just as he had no idea about my exploits with Rita, *I* had no idea just how ill prepared I was for the freedom of college life or how I would be affected by it.

CHAPTER 11

Ascending the Clock Tower

Grandma Jennie had planned for her Joseph to be a doctor, and my father expected the same for me. From the time I was a small child, it was a foregone conclusion that I would go to medical school, join his practice, and take over when he retired. "We won't even have to change the letterhead," he joked whenever we spoke about it. Dad even had me study French in high school, telling me it would help with the many Latin terms I would learn in medical school. So it came as no surprise to anyone when I enrolled in Rutgers' pre-med program. The fact that I lasted in the program for less than a semester did come as a shock, at least to my family. I wasn't all that surprised, though, considering that the only things I was studying with any regularity were the campus bars.

Other than fooling around with Rita, I'd had a very sheltered home life. Aside from school and sports, I'd rarely left the house. I never cut classes or got detention. I was a member of the National Honor Society. I barely had a sip of beer at my senior prom. So when I arrived on the Rutgers campus, it was as if I had entered a completely new world. Suddenly there were no curfews, no bans, and no one waiting to yell at me if I came in after midnight. Before long I was drinking every night and waking up with a raging hangover each morning. Rather than cutting back on the booze, I decided instead to blow off my classes. I failed calculus and was barely carrying a 2.0 GPA. I also didn't make the fall baseball team, but with my other diversions I didn't care. I was high on my newfound freedom.

I was out of control for the first time in my life except in one area: my stepmother. At college I had not only discovered the joy of drinking, but I had also finally discovered the joy of masturbation. This made it much easier to resist Rita during my visits home. We would only rendezvous a few more times before it ended for good.

When Dad got my grades in the mail, he was surprisingly calm; he didn't even make a big deal about the fact that I was no longer on the pre-med track. "Just don't flunk out," he said.

I was floored. As worried as I had been about disappointing him, his lackluster reaction to my poor grades was a thousand times worse. I had spent my entire life striving to please him only to find out he wasn't invested in my becoming a doctor after all. I had led a choirboy life for nothing. Suddenly I resented not having more fun in high school and wished I had been more like Anthony Lapadula and Frank Sardinia, the rowdy first cousins Grandma Jennie had forbade Dad from hanging out with. So what if Anthony and Frank had become landscapers? They must have had great childhoods, running around, chasing girls, and playing with slingshots. I had just learned two very painful lessons: I was not my father, and my father was certainly no Grandma Jennie.

I had always heard that college is supposed to be the best four years of your life, and like most college students I had been doing my best to make that a reality. But after learning that my father really didn't care how well I did, I began to rebel in earnest. For the next two years, I focused all my energy on making up for the time I had wasted on studying in high school. I joined a fraternity, Sig Ep, and immersed myself in all things Greek, namely, pledging, drinking, sports, and cheating on exams. I could party with the best of them, but no matter what I did or how drunk I got, I couldn't get over the feeling that I had completely missed out on my teenage years, especially when it came to girls. Sure, most of the beautiful girls at Holmdel High School had wanted my brother Stephen, but there had been some who had liked me as well. But between my father's no-dating rule and Rita's idea of motherly affection, I never had a chance to hang out with any of them. Other than my exploits with my stepmother, the furthest I had gone with a girl was kissing Suzanne Grubowski after the prom. That was one of things I set about remedying in college. The problem was I couldn't seem to buy a date at Rutgers.

In the fall of my junior year, I went with a bunch of my

fraternity brothers to the beach at Belmar, New Jersey. Some girls from the Cook campus, which was on the other side of Rutgers, came with us. They weren't bad looking, but they weren't models either. I tried hooking up with one of them at the beach. This was the same beach that my prom limo had parked on two and half years earlier. That night I had felt on top of the world as I made out with the homecoming queen. Now a girl who couldn't win the title of Dairy Queen was shooting me down. I was extremely pensive on the long ride back to Rutgers that night. I thought about my life—where I had come from and where I was going. Two days later I was trying to figure out a way to kill myself.

Two months before I descended into my first depression, Stephen and I drove out to Long Island to visit Mom, Kevin, and Beave. As we sped along the Belt Parkway and onto the Southern State, neither of us said much. It was August 1988, and in the five years since Mom had married Beave our contact with her had been limited to a handful of stilted phone conversations. But this time it wasn't fear that was making me dread the visit; it was guilt. Now almost twenty, I had started to feel bad about all the lost years and all the lies and for the simple fact that I had not fought harder to have a relationship with her or my youngest brother.

I even felt guilty about the reason for this visit. It wasn't a pleasure trip but an exchange program of sorts. Dad was throwing Grandma Jennie and Grandpa Frank a surprise fiftieth wedding anniversary party at the Shalimar Catering Hall in Staten Island and had invited all their friends and relatives from the old days. Since they had all known the family forever, there was no reason to hide Kevin like he did from the people in Holmdel. Dad wanted him at the party, but in order to get Mom's permission for this, Stephen and I had to visit her first. As usual we couldn't even see our mother unless it was part of Dad's agenda.

We pulled up to Mom's house and were greeted by a cheerful Beave holding a cooler and fishing rods. The five of us were heading out to his boat, which was docked in nearby Freeport. We spent the afternoon fishing, laughing, and having a remarkably good time. Mom was cool, Kevin was funny, and Beave was a pretty nice guy. Afterward we took separate cars to Canarsie to see Grandma Dar and Grandpa Jack. Kevin and Beave drove together, and Stephen and I rode with Mom. Unlike on previous visits, a few hours in her company seemed to wash all the years of separation away, and before we knew it we were pulling up in front of the brick house where we had spent so many happy times as children.

Before we even reached the stoop, Grandma Dar flung open the door and was standing there arms wide. She couldn't get over how much I looked like Grandpa Jack. I couldn't get over how strange I felt being in that house. I hadn't been there since disappearing from their lives more than ten years earlier.

The house hadn't changed one bit since the days when we used to drag the cot up from the basement, eat wine-soaked peaches, and watch *S.W.A.T.*, and neither had my grandparents. My grandma Dar's eyes were just as warm and loving, and her hugs were just as tight. As we sat in their living room catching up, I no longer felt distant from them.

I felt a sinking sensation in my stomach as I said good-bye

to my grandparents. Grandpa Jack was almost eighty-five, and I doubted my father would allow us to visit again anytime soon. It never dawned on me that I was old enough to sneak off from Rutgers and see my grandparents. Although I was starting to feel nostalgic and guilty, I was in many ways still in my father's grip.

From there the five of us drove to Tommaso's, a Bay Ridge restaurant known as a haven for wise guys. Beave had been introduced to the place by his brother in-law, Marty Odorisio. Marty was Beave's sister Sheila's fourth husband; he was also a disbarred lawyer with major mob ties.

Tommaso's owner liked to stroll among the tables belting out opera classics for his customers. Even better than Tommaso's voice was his food; everything, from the Caesar salad to the *spedini alla romana*, from the veal chop to the plate of *zabaglione* and strawberries—was heavenly.

I was genuinely sorry when it was time to leave. As we said good-bye, Mom and Beave gave us both Ron Chereskin sweaters that Beave had picked up at one of his sweater mills. Stephen and I were moved that they had thought to give us gifts, especially since we had rarely given them the time of day.

It was midnight by the time we got back to Holmdel. The first thing I saw when I walked into the house was Rita's angry puss, which was reminiscent of the night I blew curfew with the homecoming queen. We had left sulking earlier that day because we had no desire to visit our mother. Now we came home several hours late relaxed and full of good food, fishing tales, and new threads. Rita was livid, but she held it together...

until she heard us paying Mom a few compliments. Then she made us throw the sweaters out. Clearly her jealousy was not limited to Suzanne Grubowski. The next morning, before heading off for my junior year at Rutgers, I blew my last load on Rita.

By that time I had picked economics as my college major. I wasn't all that interested in it; instead I'd based my decision on rumors that it was easy to cheat on the Scantron exams given by the Economics Department. The professors gave the same exams year after year, and half the time we had the answers going in. The other half my fraternity brothers and I would cheat off the smartest frat brother in the class. When even that got to be too much work, I'd send a fraternity pledge to take the exam for me.

To this day I still don't know what sent me plunging into that first abyss of depression. Maybe it was all the drinking; maybe it was the realization that I had wasted my youth trying to please a crappy father and fooling around with a woman who was masquerading as my mother. Maybe it was feeling like I had missed out on all the years with Mom, Kevin, and my Paladino grandparents. No one knows for sure.

Shortly after Grandma Jennie's anniversary party, I began feeling more lethargic than normal. Two days after getting shot down by the Cook campus girl, a huge cloud began to descend over me. Already known around the frat as a world-class sleeper, my attachment to my bed became abnormal even for me. My usually healthy appetite vanished; in fact I wasn't eating at all. Within a few weeks, I lost fifteen pounds.

I stopped going to all my classes, including history, which I enjoyed. I didn't want to see or talk to anybody. I didn't shower or shave. For the first time in my life, I had a full-grown beard, and it was—of all colors—red. I might have laughed, thinking about how Grandma Jennie would have loved it, but I was too tired. I just wanted to sleep forever.

One day I finally summoned the strength to get out of bed and go to the drug store. I purchased a bottle of over-the-counter sleeping pills and took them all, hoping never to wake again. I fell asleep around midnight only to wake the next morning without so much as a headache. When medicating myself to death didn't work, I got creative. There were some fairly tall buildings on campus, and I thought about jumping from one of them. As appealing as that idea seemed, I just didn't have the balls.

Eventually a few of my frat brothers began to notice that something was wrong with me. When they asked me about it, I just shrugged. They tried to get me out of bed to go out, but I said no. I couldn't blame them for taking weeks to realize I was depressed or for not being able to help when they did finally notice. *I* didn't even know why I felt like I did, so how could they? I took only two of my five finals that semester and cheated on both of them. I did not show up for my three history exams.

Finally it was time for Christmas break. I packed my things, convinced I wouldn't live to return for the next semester. When I arrived in Holmdel, Rita and Dad took in my changed appearance and demeanor but said nothing. Later, as

I lay in bed staring listlessly at the ceiling, Dad came into my room. The first thing he said was that the beard made my face look like a crotch. When I didn't smile, he asked me what was wrong. I couldn't answer because I didn't know. I just knew I didn't want to live anymore. When Dad asked me if I thought about killing myself, I lied and told him I hadn't. I knew he was concerned, and I knew this was the first situation over which he had absolutely no control.

After a couple of days without talking or eating, it became apparent that my condition was more than just a touch of the blues. I spent the bulk of the next two weeks in bed and didn't return to Rutgers after the holidays. The Monday after New Year's, I was home alone with Rita. Before leaving for work that morning, my father had made me promise to come out of my room, so I relocated my listless, bearded self to the couch in the family room, where I quickly resumed staring off into space. I was dimly aware of Rita kicking a Nerf ball around the kitchen and adjoining family room, perhaps trying to get rid of nervous energy.

Finally, unable to take it anymore, she marched over to the couch and screamed, "Joseph, what is wrong with you?" When she realized she wasn't going to get an answer, she threw me a disgusted look. "Why won't you talk? You're making me crazy!" She didn't know what to do. She just kept kicking that ball and screaming at me. I didn't even care what she thought anymore. I just wanted to die.

A few weeks later, Dad decided it was time to consult a professional. First he had me talk to Dr. Venino, a local psychologist; I had gone to Holmdel High with his son. After we met, Dr. Venino concluded that I was depressed. No shit. He told Dad that a lot of affluent kids get depressed while in college, usually because they realize they are never going to live up to the expectations of their successful parents. In my case this had some truth. Even with the cheating, I had barely maintained a 2.5 GPA, and I had no professional ambition. Of course there was the flip side of that, which was my devastation that my father didn't care about my grades. Regardless, my behavior was clearly outside the normal college malaise. Desiring more than Venino's simplistic diagnosis, Dad took me for a second opinion, to one of the psychiatrists I had seen on Staten Island during the custody battle.

Although the psychiatrist didn't speak of the past, I wondered whether he thought all that divorce drama had finally caught up to me. In any event he too diagnosed me with depression; however, he seemed to take it more seriously than Dr. Venino. He told my father I should begin intensive psychotherapy.

That was when my father, after taking me to see two different doctors, pulled a complete about-face. I didn't need psychotherapy, he proclaimed. Instead he and Rita decided that if I wasn't going to go back to Rutgers, I should get a job. For the next several months, my depression went untreated as I returned to Avis rental cars, where I had worked the previous summer. A lot of college kids worked there during breaks, and it wasn't a bad job. Now it was the dead of winter, and everyone I knew was back in school. I didn't care, though; I was so depressed I didn't want to see anyone. I was too busy hoping

I'd get in a huge auto wreck. Some days, when I didn't want to leave it to chance, I fantasized about driving the car at a high speed into a wall. I was constantly thinking of different ways to kill myself. I even looked in my father's doctor bag for some lethal drug I could inject myself with. I didn't find anything.

One weekend the whole family went away for my brother Frank's basketball tournament. From the time he was little, Frank had been an exceptional player, probably because Rita had made me and Stephen practice with him on a daily basis. Now eleven years old, he was involved in a Biddy Basketball league that traveled all over. Whether it was Puerto Rico, Florida, or anywhere else on the planet, my Dad and Rita saw to it that Stephen and I went along for support. This time, however, because I was depressed and working at Avis, I didn't have to go. But Dad didn't want me home alone either, so he sent me to Grandma Jennie's house in Manalapan.

Normally staying at my grandparents' was cause for celebration, but this time I didn't even care. Until, that is, I remembered the shotgun Grandpa Frank had purchased in Old Forge during that one visit in the late 1970s. One night, after my grandparents went to bed, I went looking for the gun in the basement. I was not going to kill myself in their house, but I was planning to take it. I tore the basement apart, but the gun was nowhere to be found. I later learned that Grandma Jennie had made my grandfather get rid of it when they moved from Staten Island. There is little doubt in my mind that had I found the gun that winter, I would have used it to blow my head off.

This inability to find the appropriate suicide method can

be seen as miraculous or humorous depending on how one looks at it. In any event it would happen with every bout of depression over the next two dozen years. I'm not good with knots, so I couldn't hang myself. I don't like the sight of blood, so I would never slit my wrists. I never crashed my car because I figured with my luck I'd end up a quadriplegic and never be able to finish the job. Then there were the times I didn't even have the strength to get out of bed let alone do myself bodily harm. Some might think this means I'm not serious, but I can say without reservation that when I am depressed I really do want to die. In fact if there had been a button I could press next to my bed or a cocked and loaded gun within reach, I would have been dead years ago.

CHAPTER 12

Cabron Loco

As the winter turned into spring, the cloud began to lift. Before I had fallen into depression in November, I had booked a trip to Acapulco for spring break along with forty of my fraternity brothers. Since I was feeling better and had already paid for the trip, Dad thought it would do me some good to go. He asked the shrink, who agreed.

I headed to Rutgers a few days before we were scheduled to leave. A few of the guys were going to the tanning salon to get a base so they wouldn't burn in the hot Mexican sun, and I decided to join them. The bright lights in the tanning bed further lifted my mood, and by the time we boarded the plane I was feeling much more like myself. In fact after a few hours on the beach in Acapulco, I started feeling really fucking good.

Of all places to experience one's first mania, I had mine in a country known for its subhuman jails. And it was truly a miracle that I did not end up in one of them. I spent my days drinking, arm wrestling for money, chasing girls, threatening Mexicans, and basically acting like a total imbecile. Unable to sleep for more than an hour at a time, I spent my nights much the same way. I was having a blast. I hadn't been that high on life since that last Christmas Eve at Shangri-La. I even called Grandma Jennie from Acapulco to tell her I felt like a million bucks. For a kid who never said much, I suddenly couldn't shut up. Grandma Jennie couldn't believe how much I was talking, but she was thrilled I was feeling better. But when she called Dad to tell him the good news, he didn't share her relief; in fact he was more concerned than ever. What his mother was describing sounded an awful lot like mania.

However, I had no clue. I spent the rest of the week burning through my money and talking incessantly to anyone who would listen. I assumed everything—including my lack of sleep—was a combination of the excitement of spring break and tequila. My luck with women had magically transformed as well. At Rutgers they had treated me like a leper. Now, tanned, cut, and sporting balls the size of Texas, I was hooking up with gorgeous girls every night.

Toward the end of the week, I met a beautiful girl from New Jersey. Unfortunately she was going home the next day. I offered Ira Brassloff, a frat brother of mine, a thousand dollars to switch flights with her so she could travel with me a few days later. That whole night at the bar, I was screaming, "Ira is going home tomorrow!" Ira was going to do it, but the girl chickened out, fearing the airline wouldn't go for it. She left the next day but invited me to a party in Jersey the following week.

I had brought a thousand dollars with me on the trip, which was quite a bit of money for Mexico circa 1989. I had saved every dime I'd earned at Avis because other than for work, I never left the house. Otherwise I had never been particularly shrewd with money. My father's free-spending habits had rubbed off on me, plus he had always given my brothers and me plenty of money. I was never short of cash; in fact the guys at the frat house were envious that I could go out to dinner every night, sometimes ordering two meals at a sitting.

What I was experiencing in Acapulco was outrageous even for me. I was determined to spend every last dollar I had brought. Still, despite buying rounds at the bar and eating two steak dinners every night, I couldn't spend it all. I had won hundreds of dollars arm wrestling guys in the bars. I felt like giving it all away. Finally, with the end of the week approaching, I started giving taxicab drivers huge tips. Sometimes they would take me only fifty feet, and I would tell them to let me out. I would literally throw the money at them. They didn't know whether to curse me for being obnoxious or thank me for giving them a month's pay. One saluted me with his middle finger and shouted, "*Cabron loco!*"

He was right. I was a crazy motherfucker. Still in the grip of full-blown mania, I flew back to New Jersey. Already on high alert after speaking to Grandma Jennie, my father's suspicions were confirmed after I took Frank and Matthew for a drive. When they told Dad how I was swerving off the road and zooming around trees in a nearby park, he promptly forbade them from getting in the car with me. After burying his head in the sand for months, he finally realized something had to be done before someone ended up dead.

When my father told me I was sick and had to go to the hospital, I thought *he* was nuts. I had been nearly catatonic for the previous five months, and no one had ever mentioned hospitalization. Now that I was feeling better than ever, they wanted to put me away? I didn't want to go anywhere but back to the fraternity house at Rutgers. I also had a date lined up the next night with the beautiful girl from Acapulco.

It was no use arguing; my father had made up his mind. He and Rita checked me in to the Princeton House, the first and nicest of the dozen and a half or so hospitals to which I would be admitted over the next two decades. Located in idyllic Princeton, New Jersey, it was the country club of mental hospitals, serving the needs of affluent, drug-addicted youths. It had a workout room, cable television, beautiful grounds, and a dessert menu. It would have been a relatively pleasant stay had I not made the first of many poor manic decisions while I was there.

It had been easy to convince my frat brothers that my parents were crazy and had wrongfully checked me in to a hospital. In no time a few pledges drove down to Princeton and picked me up. The Princeton House was not a locked unit. I simply walked out the front door. As the night nurse begged me to stay, my frat brothers and I broke into song—"Na na na na.... Na na na na.... Hey hey hey.... Good-bye"—before speeding off toward Rutgers.

We were there no more than a half hour when Dad, Grandpa Frank, and a very pissed off Rita came barging in. My father and grandfather just stood there as Rita started screaming at every guy in the frat house. "Don't you know he is sick? How dare anyone check him out of the hospital!" I had never seen her so angry; even her post-homecoming rage paled in comparison. She even blasted some poor bastard who had nothing to do with my escape.

Like all of Rita's meltdowns, the real reason behind this one became apparent after the fact. Like my father, Rita was in the medical field and surely recognized mania when she saw it. She also knew how unpredictable and loose-lipped manics are. I was a walking, talking time bomb, set to spill our secret at any second.

I eventually left with them, but not before telling them unequivocally that there was no way I was going back to Princeton House. They agreed. Princeton House was definitely not the place for me. Instead they'd be taking me to Staten Island Hospital the next morning. I was furious but managed to hold my tongue until we got home. Then, as soon as I got Rita alone, I informed her that if I missed the date I would fuck the shit out of her. That must have gotten her attention, and she must have gotten to my father, because later he told me I didn't have to check in to Staten Island hospital; I just had to meet with the doctors there. If they thought I was okay, I could come home. Convinced that I was fine and Dad and Rita were crazy, I agreed to go.

The next day at the hospital, I met with a psychiatrist named Dr. Adler. I would eventually grow fond of him both as an individual and as a professional; however, on the day of our first meeting, when he diagnosed me with manic depression and told me I needed to be admitted, I thought he was suffering from the same insanity as Dad and Rita. Manic depression, Adler explained, is caused by a chemical imbalance in the brain. What causes that chemical imbalance is not known. While there is evidence that genetics plays a part, the doctor added, it is not known what can trigger its onset. I would later learn that traumatic childhoods are a common thread among those with this illness. But in that first meeting, at Dad's insistence Adler repeated the genetic component to bipolar. It would be Dad's first attempt at insulating himself from any responsibility, but it would not be his last.

When I was in the depression phase, I would have loved to know what was wrong with me. Now, high on mania, I didn't care to debate the etiology of my illness. I felt great and just wanted out of there. When Adler finished speaking, I laughed and calmly made my way toward the exit. I had walked out of Princeton House. I figured I could do the same here.

When I realized I was in a locked unit and was not getting out for my date, I became enraged. I charged at Dr. Adler but was overwhelmed by seven orderlies. It took them several minutes to get me down. When they finally got my left arm pinned, I laughed.

"I'm right handed, assholes," I told them.

They still got the last laugh when the nurse hit me in the ass with a shot of Thorazine.

I woke up in four-points position a day and a half later. That Thorazine is some strong shit, and when I wasn't comatose I was hallucinating. I stared in awe as monkeys did flips on the ceiling of my rubber room. Since I felt like a monkey in a cage, this made perfect sense. The staff placed an older security guard in my room to watch me. He knew Dad, who had been on staff there for years, and told me if I didn't give him any trouble he would untie my hands. I told him he didn't have to worry. I didn't have the energy to fart.

Dr. Adler started me on a course of lithium, the "wonder drug" for manic depression. Developed in the 1950s, it had brought hope to the thousands of bipolar sufferers who previously had no success with medication. Lithium is a natural salt that, taken in the right dose, is very successful at alleviating the chemical imbalance and the accompanying highs and lows. Still, like any other medical treatment, it is not a panacea. Not everyone takes well to lithium. It has side effects such as diarrhea, acne, dry mouth, decreased libido, and kidney dysfunction.

Dr. Adler explained that given my age, size, and metabolism—not to mention my severe mania—I would need a very high dose. As a result I developed diarrhea and acne on my back. Worse still the medication took forever to work. The staff kept promising me I was going to be released. But one week soon turned into two with no significant improvement. A month later I was still in the hospital.

Highly agitated, I had little patience for anyone, particularly the gay guy two rooms down from me. Each morning he appeared at my door singing, "It's time to get up in the morning, the morning. It's time to get up in the morning." I wanted to kill him. Sometimes he would come into my room and lie on top of me to wake me up. One morning I awoke before he got there. I kept my eyes shut, pretending to be asleep as he approached my bed, then when he got close enough I jumped up and threw him across the room. The guy nearly shit in his pants. After that he stopped coming to my room, and I never heard him sing the song again.

Even worse than the agitation was the boredom. When depressed, I loved to lie around all day, sleeping and contemplating death. Mania is a completely different animal, and when I was manic I was a completely different person. Filled with boundless, delusional energy, I wanted to be out spending money, meeting women, and doing any outrageous thing that caught my attention.

My only relief came in the form of Mike Miccio, a powerfully built forty-three-year-old who was involuntarily admitted to the locked unit after New York's finest found him hanging off the ledge of the Verrazano Bridge. Mike had threatened to jump, but he had not been trying to kill himself; in fact he had been so high he believed he could jump off the 350-foot high bridge and survive. His ultimate goal in attempting this feat was to get into the *Guinness Book of World Records* or, as Mike called it, the *McGuiness Book of World Records*.

Mike was not the most educated person around, but thanks to a hard-knocks education in Bensonhurst, Brooklyn, he was as street smart as they come. He was also one of the most larger-than-life characters I'd ever met. Mike and I hit it off from the start, which wasn't so surprising considering we were both high as kites and everyone else on the unit was drugged up or pathologically boring. When I told him I had just been diagnosed with bipolar, he said, "Kid, you're in for the hassle of your life."

The past six months flashed before me, and I knew I had just heard the biggest understatement since Kevin referred to the Beave's lips as "big." Within minutes Mike and I had told each other our life stories including those personal things you don't usually tell someone you've just met. For example he told me he had a "horse cock," and I told him about the thing with Rita. He was impressed but said I should have slept with her.

"I would have taken care of her," he said, gesturing to his crotch.

Already pissed off that he had been locked up, Mike was even more furious when the *Staten Island Advance* reported that a "despondent man" from the New Dorp section of Staten Island had been "rescued" from the Verrazano Bridge. Determined to get them to retract that story, he had his wife, Susan, bring him a roll of quarters for the pay phone. He had me calling the police precinct and the newspaper all afternoon. He wanted them to get the story straight. He had not been trying to kill himself. He was just trying to make the record books.

Mike was only too happy to take me under his wing. A longstanding veteran of bipolar, he was a regular face around the locked unit of Staten Island Hospital. In fact the psychiatric staff had been studying his entire family for years. Bipolar had literally torn the Miccios apart; Mike's brother and sister had been diagnosed as well as several aunts and uncles. His brother had earned minor celebrity status after a daring but unsuccessful escape attempt from the very same unit Mike and I were now in. In a fit of manic desperation, he had smashed a window and jumped to the courtyard below. His plan had one major flaw, however: the courtyard was also locked. He wouldn't have gotten too far even if he hadn't broken his leg in the fall.

I hadn't been all that interested when Dr. Adler told me about the genetic aspect of the disease, but in Mike I had a living, breathing example, and a fascinating one at that. When he wasn't in four-point restraints, he was running around the streets of Brooklyn and Staten Island, committing low-level crimes and generally raising hell with his band of wannabe mobsters. Whenever he got into trouble with the law, which was quite often, one never knew whether it was his mania or his love for the thug life. However, when his neighbors called 911 because of his erratic behavior, the cops knew to bring him straight to the hospital.

Mike told me all about the staff and their routines, explaining that no matter how big or strong or filled with super-human mania I was, I'd still be no match for the 140-pound shrink armed with a hypodermic needle.

"With one injection he'll turn you into a friggin' zombie," Mike said, making a plunging gesture with an imaginary syringe.

Mike lived in perpetual fear that the doctors would give him a lobotomy, but I never knew whether that was the mania talking or if he had seen *One Flew Over the Cuckoo's Nest* too many times.

There was one thing that Mike couldn't tell me too much about, and that was depression. Fortunately for him he rarely experienced the side of the disease where he wanted to kill himself or just sleep the rest of his life away. When he was hospitalized, it was almost always for some manic—and probably fun—escapade. Now that I knew both the soul-crushing depression and the euphoric rush of the mania, I couldn't help feeling envious of him.

Like most manics, busting chops was one of Mike's favorite pastimes, and he was always looking for an opportunity to abuse the staff. When they decided a few days later to transfer him to the other side of the hospital, he disappeared into thin air.

"It's a locked unit," I reminded them with a snicker. "Where's he gonna go?"

It took them over an hour to find him hiding in the shower.

I was disappointed to see Mike go; my father, on the other hand, was relieved. The staff had told him about Miccio's history, and he probably figured I was crazy enough without hanging out with a fellow manic, not to mention one with a criminal record.

Prince DeBlasi. Our father in Canarsie, 1943.

Approximate ages when Dad walked out: Steve at one and a half years, Joe at three years, and Kevin at ten months.

Grandma Dar, Kevin, Steve, Joe, and Grandpa Jack in Canarsie, 1974.

Brothers at the pool.

Steve, Joe, and Kevin enjoying brotherhood.

Kevin, Steve, and Joe share a bath.

Mom, Aunt Paula, Kevin, Joe, and Steve during the first post-custody visit. Statue of Liberty, Spring 1979.

Lake George, summer 1976.

Mom and David Karmi, Halloween 1977.

Ready for trick-or-treating.

Joe joining the a cappella group at Steve's wedding, September 1998.

Kevin, Grandma Dar, and Joe, September 1998.

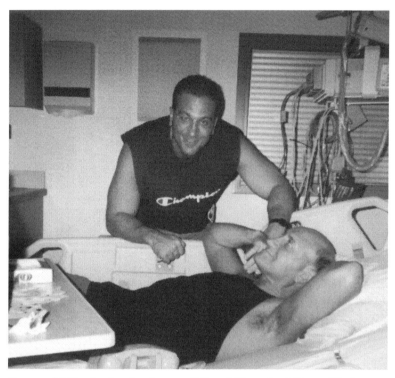

Joe and Miccio in the Staten Island Hospital Burn Unit, September 1998.

Joe, June 2000.

Mom and Dad.

Mom, Grandpa Jack, Grandma Jenny, and Dad.

Joe and his godfather, Grandpa Frank.
Confirmation, May 1979.

Beave.

Joe at the time of the
life-altering taxicab ride.

CHAPTER 13

From Coal to Diamonds

At the start of my stay, Dad visited every day. He'd either make
the short drive over from his office or pop in to the locked
unit after seeing patients in other parts of the hospital. While
I was still angry with him for having me committed, I looked
forward to the break in the monotony, especially after Mike
was moved.

Then I began to notice that he was acting differently toward
me. It was fairly subtle; he didn't joke around like he used to,
and he seemed to be avoiding direct eye contact. I had no idea
what was going on until the day Dr. Adler told me about an
interesting conversation he'd had with my father. Rita, afraid
that I would divulge our secret in therapy, had decided to
spill the beans first. Of course she took artistic license, telling
my father that over the past few years I had been physically

accosting her. She had tried to fight me off, but I was just too strong. The "harassment" had culminated with my threat to "fuck the shit out of her" right before I was hospitalized. She hadn't said anything to my father before because she was afraid he'd throw me out.

Initially Dr. Adler surmised that my sexual aggression toward Rita had been early manifestations of mania. Then he heard *my* side of the story. After I had recovered from the shock of Rita's revelation, I told Dr. Adler everything beginning with how Rita used to wash my hair when I visited the Grasmere house as a young boy. I told him how in the early 1980s my thank-you kisses had turned into passionate make out sessions. I told him that as I got older I did initiate the contact, but contrary to what Rita had told my father, she only pretended to resist. As I spoke I doubted Dr. Adler would believe me; after all I was the one locked up in the loony bin, and Rita was a nurse and the wife of a highly respected physician. I figured if anything, Adler would up my dose of lithium then lock me up and throw away the key. Except he didn't. He not only believed my story, he explained to me that because the kissing had started when I was so young, I was not responsible for my actions as I got older. I had nothing to feel guilty about; the fault was entirely Rita's.

They say God works in mysterious ways. Well, luckily for me, manic depression does too. Under normal circumstances my father's finding out about the affair would have completely destroyed me. Regardless of Rita's role, I would have been on my knees crying and begging for his forgiveness. However, when the story broke, I was still manic and preoccupied with getting out of the hospital. This cushioned me from a lot of the emotional upheaval I would have experienced if I were on an even keel, not to mention if I were depressed. If that had been the case, I would have been the one jumping out the window and not with the intention of breaking out of the hospital.

My father had an even stranger reaction to the news of my trysts with Rita. He flatly refused to believe that she had any culpability despite the fact that she was an adult and I had been a child, despite her convenient, eleventh-hour confession. If Rita had wanted to put an end to the kissing and touching, she could have simply said, "Stop it or I'm going to tell your six-foot-four, three-hundred-pound father," and I never would have laid another hand on her. Even Dr. Adler told Dad he was burying his head in the sand. The revelation that his young wife was fooling around with his son must have come as a tremendous blow, and everyone who knew my father thought this denial was completely out of character for him. Yet deny it he did, and he continues to do so to this day.

My father might have been able to ignore the truth about his wife, but he couldn't continue to ignore the truth about me. He had allowed me to wallow in my depression for months; however, now that I was in the hospital he was forced to deal with it. At Dr. Adler's insistence, he and Rita finally agreed to attend a family counseling session with Thomas DiMartini, a therapist at the hospital. The session lasted about a half hour and was completely useless. Very little was said, especially by Rita, who was as white as a ghost. In the end, though, she had nothing to worry about because her gamble had paid off. Whatever my father really believed, he remained steadfastly in her corner. However, he also let me return to his house after my release from the hospital, which was particularly odd since, according to Rita, I had physically overpowered her for years. Needless to say when I arrived in Holmdel after seven weeks away, I was not greeted with open arms.

As I would soon learn, my father was dealing with other crises as well: Kevin, who was finishing up his last year of high school, had been accepted to the University of Pennsylvania. When he told my father, Dad congratulated him, then generously offered him $5,000 toward the tuition. This was a joke, and everyone knew it. UPenn was an Ivy League school. Its tuition was running well over twenty grand a year. Mom and Beave weren't going to take this lying down. They consulted Saul Edelstien, a hotshot family lawyer who had been recommended to them by Beave's brother-in-law, Marty. Edelstien explained that my father was bound to pay a portion of Kevin's tuition commensurate with his income.

Claiming he couldn't afford to pay more, Dad hired his old friend LeMole to represent him. In court Beave pointed out that I had applied to UPenn just a few years earlier. Since my father's income hadn't decreased since then, he couldn't very well cry pauper now that Kevin was going there. The judge agreed. Dad lost the case and was ordered to pay $15,000 a year. It was a sweet and long-overdue victory for Mom, and Beave, ecstatic that he had wiped the floor with LeMole, told everyone what an excellent attorney he would have made.

Kevin, who had hoped Dad was finally going to do right by him, was disgusted that he'd had to sue his own father for college tuition. Determined never to be hurt again by Dad, Kevin severed all ties with him.

My father wasn't being completely dishonest about his financial situation, however. His showy lifestyle had finally begun to catch up with him, especially his Holmdel palace. At more than seven thousand square feet, it cost a small fortune just to heat the place. Even before Kevin's lawsuit, Dad and Rita had discussed putting it on the market; after the lawsuit it became a necessity. In the end they had spent more time waiting for the house to be built than they had actually lived in it. The sad truth was he couldn't really afford the house in the first place; half the rooms had remained empty the whole time. The gossips in Holmdel must have had a field day when it went on the selling block, especially since Jon Bon Jovi was one of the potential buyers. He was looking for a place for his parents. When he told Dad he had decided to buy a place in Rumson, New Jersey, instead, Dad quipped, "What, do you want to be like Springsteen?" Evidently my father had kept abreast of where New Jersey rockers liked to live. He wound up selling the house for nearly $2 million, which he used to build a more modest house in Holmdel.

After I was released from the hospital, it was time to figure out what my next step was. One of Dad's patients, Tony Gerace, was a trader for the Wall Street brokerage house of Herzog, Heinz and Gudold, and he hired me for the summer. Gerace was a solid guy and an avid sports fan, and since he didn't have athletic sons of his own, he loved spending time with our family.

Working at Herzog was neither difficult nor interesting. The hour-and-a- half commute from Holmdel to lower Manhattan was hell. I was still on a high dose of lithium and suffered from acne, dry mouth, and severe diarrhea. Fortunately there was a bathroom on the bus.

Even with the medication, I was still slightly manic that summer. I had always been a quiet, laid-back guy, but that person was gone, replaced by a confident—even arrogant—one. I wasn't out of control like I had been in Acapulco, but I had a sarcastic, ballsy demeanor that I absolutely loved. One day I was on my way home from work and grateful that I had found a seat in the back of the packed bus. As we pulled away from a stop, a man who had just gotten on weaved down the aisle, looking for a seat. When he asked me whether there were any seats in the back, I calmly pointed to the toilet to my right. Not amused, the man muttered something under his breath, then turned around and stood for the rest of the trip. Had I not been feeling high, I would not even have made eye contact with the man, so despite the side effects, I was extremely grateful the lithium allowed me to feel so good.

Dad and Rita were far less pleased with my new personality. The Joe DeBlasi they knew had always done whatever he was told; now they figured I'd still be on my best behavior, especially since my "crimes" against Rita had come out. None of that mattered to the new Joe, though. To add insult to injury, I gave Mike Miccio our phone number.

Mike continued to be fascinated by my physical relationship with Rita. Whenever we spoke of it, he wanted to know every detail even though I had told him many times before. Every time he had the same responses: "Joey, you were the luckiest thirteen-year-old kid around." "Joey, I can't believe you didn't fuck her." "Joey, I bet your kid brother Kevin would have." Even as a grown man, Mike viewed the situation through the eyes of a kid; in fact to this day, he fails to see how wrong—not to mention damaging— it is to hook up with your stepmother on a daily basis. According to Mike I didn't need to date in high school because I had "the built-in pound."

Miccio called the house quite a bit depending on how manic he was and loved when Rita answered the phone. One day, after he told Rita he had an uncircumcised cock and asked whether she wanted to try it out, my father demanded that I stop speaking with him. That was only one of the new ground rules. My father was laying down the law on several fronts. We couldn't walk around in our underwear anymore. Frank and Matthew, who were still just kids, could not lie in bed with Rita. After being asleep at the wheel for years, Dad was now hypersensitive when it came to his wife and teenage boys— even her biological sons.

One day my high school friend Danny Chow came over to hang out. I don't know if Chow meant to kiss Rita on the lips or if she accidentally turned the wrong way, but my father was pissed. "What, does everyone around here want my wife?" he snarled, unable to believe that some teenage "chink" had taken liberties with Rita right in front of him. I wanted to throw up.

Things around the house were certainly tense, and I didn't even have Stephen to commiserate with. He was at the University of Georgia, where he had been accepted on a baseball scholarship. That didn't mean he had escaped the family drama, however, because I was about to pull him back in. Unlike me, Stephen hadn't accepted Dad's no-dating edict; in fact all through high school he had been sneaking out to meet girls. By the time he'd begun his senior year, he'd already had a serious girlfriend, and each night after Dad went to bed Steve would slip out of the house, grab his bike, and ride over to her house.

When I was the old Joe, I never would have ratted my brother out. Now, manic and pissed that I had never had the balls to defy my father, I told Dad about Stephen's secret social life. Stephen returned home after his freshman year and unknowingly walked into a shit storm. Although he knew I had been depressed over the winter, no one had told him about my mania and subsequent hospitalization. He was also unaware that I had squealed about his nocturnal escapades the year before.

One would think the statute of limitations had run out on Stephen's high school dating defiance, but my father had reached the end of his patience. Thanks to me Stephen had to endure a loud, seemingly never-ending lecture. As if this weren't punishment enough, my father told him he couldn't drive the 1986 Trans Am Stephen and I shared. My relationship with Rita and Stephen's sneaking around had taught him one thing, however: dating bans weren't the way to go. My half brothers, Frank and Matthew, would be spared that particular rule.

My father had to admit that his family was disintegrating before his very eyes. My therapist, Thomas DiMartini, had been trying all summer to get us into family counseling sessions, but thanks to Rita and Dad's reluctance, it hadn't happened. Now, with Stephen back from school, they finally gave in.

It was the day of the appointment. The car was quiet as the four of us headed to Staten Island—well, quiet except for the sound of me busting everyone's chops. I noticed that Rita was carrying a brown shopping bag but had no idea what was in it. Looking back, it was probably better that I didn't or all hell would have broken loose on the Staten Island Expressway.

We had barely sat down in DiMartini's office when Rita opened the bag. Then, with the flair of a prosecutor with the smoking gun, she pulled out several pairs of men's underwear. For a moment the room was silent as the men tried to figure out their significance.

"You see what I have to deal with?" she said, waving them around as if that explained everything. That was when I realized they were my underpants, and they were soiled.

DiMartini looked at her questioningly.

"He's a lazy slob," she spat, pointing a pair of tighty-whities in my direction, "who can't even be bothered to wipe his own ass. And why should he when I'm around to pick these up off the floor and wash them?"

It was Rita's way of saying that taking care of a manic depressive was not easy. But if she was looking for sympathy, she had the wrong man. DiMartini had been doing this a long time, and he was no fool. He knew that Rita was merely trying to deflect attention from the real issue—our incestuous relationship and how it might have affected my mental health. By the time he got a chance to broach the topic, our time was nearly up. My father and Rita said they'd return the following week, but it was an empty promise. It would be our last family counseling session.

By the fall of 1989, I was ready to return to Rutgers. I had continued to see DiMartini over the summer, and between our sessions and a constant flow of lithium, I was feeling good. I was also sick of waking up at the crack of dawn and commuting two hours into the city for a minimum-wage job. I didn't waste any time when I got back to Rutgers, and I'm not talking about academics. Although I was a semester behind, I resumed my role as a full-time frat brother—skipping classes, cheating on exams, playing sports, and drinking beer. Having experienced a severe depression and an extreme high, my courses seemed more trivial than ever.

Still new to the world of bipolar, I had yet to recognize another running theme of the illness: these highs and lows render *all* aspects of normal life unimportant. School, work, finances, relationships, and my future suddenly didn't faze me. When you have been so depressed that you lie in bed for months thinking of ways to kill yourself, everything else pales in comparison. Moreover, when you've been manic and feeling pretty close to omnipotent, the thought of getting a C on an exam or getting fired from a bullshit job doesn't rate either.

One thing I had realized early on, however, was that I loved being Manic Joe. I had spent the first twenty years of my life conforming to what my father and society dictated: study hard, behave, stand in line, wait your turn, be courteous and polite. Manic Joe didn't worry about these things. He did whatever he wanted with no apprehension or inhibitions. When I had been normal, I was so docile I wouldn't even question a dinner bill twenty dollars in the proprietor's favor. When manic I thought nothing of going into a restaurant and ordering a five-course meal even if I had no money (something I would actually do many years later in Atlantic City). It's like having a dynamic alter ego, like Superman and Clark Kent. This feeling was exacerbated by the fact that other than the hopelessness and the desire to kill myself, my depressed state was much closer to my normal personality.

By the winter of 1989, my condition had stabilized. I didn't know whether the medication had finally kicked in or it was just time for my brain chemistry to be back in balance, but I was pretty much back to my old self. Manic Joe had disappeared.

Things at home were far from normal, however. When I came home from school for the holidays, I learned I would be allowed to stay only for the actual holiday. After we ate, Stephen drove me back to school. Even as I looked around the empty fraternity house, it never occurred to me to reach out to my mother. I hadn't seen her since Stephen and I went on that fishing trip, and she knew nothing of my illness. After all that had gone on between us, there was no way I was making *that* phone call.

With no family to speak of, I immersed myself in my

friends and fraternity activities. As the end of the school year approached, I began considering my options for the summer break. My father had not told me I couldn't come home, but after I was cast out over the holidays it was patently clear that I wasn't wanted. The previous summer a few of my fraternity brothers had rented a house in Belmar on the Jersey Shore. It had been a blast, so when they said they could get me a job at Bar Anticipation, I immediately took them up on it. "Bar A" was one of the largest indoor-outdoor nightclubs in the tristate area, and, true to their word, my frat brothers landed me a job as a bouncer.

Going to Belmar was one of the best decisions of my life. I met more girls in one night at Bar A than I had in four years at Rutgers. I wasn't sure, but I suspected it was the Bar A shirt I had to wear while working. The shirt had magical properties similar to the stethoscope Dad wore at Maimonides: it was a magnet for women. I could have been a cyclops and I still would have hooked up.

A few weeks into the summer, I met Kerri, an attractive, intelligent girl from Missouri who was studying—of all things—to be a psychiatric nurse. She had taken a summer job waitressing at a nearby nightclub but had the added perk of studying me. Kerri wasn't the first girl I had slept with, but she was my first girlfriend. We dated for the remainder of the summer and stayed in touch even after she went back to Missouri.

I returned to Rutgers in the fall of 1990 just four classes shy of my diploma. Many of my fraternity brothers had graduated the previous May, but I quickly found other people to hang with. I broke my foot quarterbacking in a fraternity football game, but my injury did nothing to slow down my partying. Five or six nights a week, I could be found in the campus bars expertly navigating the crowds with my crutches.

Around December, just as I felt myself sliding back into a depression, I received a phone call that would become a turning point in my life. It was my brother Kevin calling me from his dorm room at the University of Pennsylvania. He had gotten my number from Grandma Jennie.

After hearing that Dad had made me return to Rutgers on Christmas Day, Grandma Jennie had confronted him. She couldn't imagine what had happened to make him treat the apple of his eye that way. When pressed, Dad blurted, "In my house, he put the moves on my wife!"

At first Grandma Jennie had no idea what he was talking about. When she figured it out, she was sick to her stomach. She hadn't been that nauseated since she had witnessed Rita's dog eating its feces back in Old Forge.

My father was kidding himself to think that Grandma Jennie would buy his version of the story. Some of the sharpest tax attorneys in Manhattan hadn't been able to fool her, so she wasn't going to be duped by the coalminer's daughter. Like Dr. Adler and Thomas DiMartini, my grandmother knew the responsibility for our relationship lie with Rita.

"It takes two to tango," Grandpa Frank remarked when she told him.

The only thing my grandmother couldn't figure out was

why my father was standing by her. After careful consideration she finally concluded that "Rita must have a crotch of diamonds."

Once again Rita had driven a wedge between Grandma Jennie and "her Joseph." He had chosen Rita over his parents back in the early '80s, and now he was choosing her over his son. When my father told her that he planned to wash his hands of me after I graduated college, it was the final straw. Grandma Jennie and Grandpa Frank decided it was time to get Kevin and Mom back into my life.

Nearly three years had passed since I had seen or spoken to Kevin. He had wanted to reach out to me and Stephen but was afraid we were mad at him for suing Dad. Kevin had no idea about everything else that had happened since then. Grandma Jennie didn't tell him—maybe she thought it wasn't her place.

Other than letting Kevin know there were no hard feelings about the lawsuit, I kept the conversation light. I didn't say anything about my illness or my falling out with our father. Even though I was on Dad's shit list, I was also still under his influence. He had made it clear that I was not to talk about my manic depression, and he certainly didn't want me telling people I had spent my teenage years hooking up with his wife.

It might not have been true confessions, but it was great just talking to Kevin again. We spoke about college life and reminisced about the great vacations we had taken together over the years. One of our favorite places was Club Med in Bermuda, which we had visited back in 1987. When I mentioned that I would be graduating that January but didn't have any career plans or ambitions, Kevin suggested I apply to a Club Med resort. "You'll get more ass than a toilet seat," he kept saying. He had always been a pisser, but now he was achieving the impossible—making me laugh while I was depressed. With no idea about my illness, and assuming I was still close with Dad, he didn't ask me to get together. I didn't suggest a meeting either. I had truly enjoyed hearing from him, but I was already spiraling downward and didn't want to see anybody. Missing one another, we said our good-byes and hung up.

A few weeks later, depressed and suicidal, I graduated from Rutgers. There were no celebrations or gifts, but I did receive a surprise from my father. He informed me that under "the circumstances," I was going to have to "take one for the team." This meant I was no longer welcome in his house or his life. He couldn't deal with what happened between Rita and me, he said, so one of us had to go. That someone wasn't going to be Rita and her crotch of diamonds. As a consolation prize, he gave me his old Cadillac and the nearly $2,000 that had been in a bank account under Kevin's name. Kevin had gotten the money for birthdays and holidays over the years, but Dad had never let him take it back to Mom's house. To add insult to injury, Dad suggested I get a job at McDonald's. After years of saying how we would be partners in a medical practice, the cruelty of this remark could not have escaped him, not to mention the fact that he was throwing his suicidal son out into the street when it could very likely be a death sentence.

Worse yet he still discouraged me from reaching out to my mother for fear that the Rita situation would be exposed.

Homeless and despondent, it was a miracle I didn't kill myself. I was not just a lost boy; I was a lost soul.

Without a home, a job, or the will to live, I packed up my things and grabbed the first train to St. Louis. Kerri, my girlfriend from the previous summer, had invited me to live with her and her mother. As my father and I parted ways, he got in one last dig: "Don't hook up with the mother."

The trip to Missouri was interminable. I spent the entire time praying the train would derail and I would be killed. When I finally got to Kerri's house, she took one look at me and knew something was very wrong. It wasn't that she didn't want to help, she said, but she was out of her depth. I'd be better off getting treated by my doctors on Staten Island.

One day after arriving in the Show Me State, I was showing myself back to New York. I promised Kerri I would not harm myself and would check in to a hospital as soon as I arrived. A man of my word, I did just that, but it took every ounce of restraint not to end my life by jumping on the train tracks. I spent the next few months under Dr. Adler's care at Staten Island Hospital.

My condition did nothing to soften my father's heart. He still wanted nothing to do with me, and, unlike during my first hospitalization, didn't visit once. Fortunately Grandma Jennie and Grandpa Frank did come to see me. When my father found out, he gave them an ultimatum: if they took me in after my release from the hospital, he would stop speaking to them for good.

As always my father had an agenda. He knew full well that Grandma Jennie and Grandpa Frank would never let their grandson be turned out on the street. The threat was just an excuse to cut ties with his parents, which he had wanted to do ever since they made it clear how they felt about Rita's role in our trysts.

"I don't go for this shit," my grandmother told him. "It's nonsense that Rita didn't know how to stop it."

"It takes two to tango," Grandpa Frank reiterated.

Enraged, my father insisted they had always had it in for Rita and were just looking to pin something on her.

In the end it all worked according to plan. When my grandparents refused to abandon me, my father cut them out of his life. And he didn't stop there; he also severed ties with his brother, my uncle Mike, as well as Aunt Kathy and practically every other member of his extended family.

CHAPTER 14

Beach Blanket Mania

When I was released from Staten Island Hospital in April 1991, my grandparents were waiting for me with open arms. The first month at their house went pretty well; I was stable on my meds and spent most of my time watching TV and eating like a king. In fact I was feeling so normal that when my friends at Rutgers asked me to hang out for a weekend, I figured, what's the harm? That was when I learned another lesson: alcohol interferes with the delicate balance that often takes months of lithium and therapy to achieve. After just a few days of partying, I was high as a kite, and soon I had burned right through the severance pay from Dad.

For the first time in my life, I was short on cash, and not even Grandma Jennie could come to my rescue. My grandparents, it turned out, had been dealing with their own problems.

A few years earlier, Grandpa Frank had been arrested under the federal RICO statute. Apparently my seventy-five-year-old grandfather thought it was a good idea to go in on a little business deal with a "connected" cousin.

Unfortunately the investment was in marijuana, and the Mafioso cousin was under FBI surveillance. The feds had tapes of Grandpa Frank buying in to the deal as he and his cousin rode around Atlantic City in a limo; he had even referred to the "weed." He hired Paul LeMole to defend him, who managed to get him off with community service at the local library. He was supposed to return books to the shelves, but he was so confused by the Dewey Decimal System that the head librarian decided he'd do less damage at the front counter. Grandpa Frank also had to pay a large fine, and between that and LeMole's enormous legal fees, he had done some real damage to his and Grandma Jennie's nest egg. My brothers and I were never comfortable asking either of them more about it; however, we had no doubt that she wanted to kill him.

It was the worst possible time for them to have me living there, especially once the mania really kicked in. I was ravenous, eating as if every meal were my last, and contributed nothing to the household expenses. I had resumed working at Bar A that summer, but most of my money was going to the rented beach house I had gone in on with the other bouncers as well as the speeding tickets I racked up every time I drove between Manalapan and Belmar. I would have gotten even more, but whenever I told the local cops where I worked they let me off the hook. Bar A was a big police hang out. If I were normal, I simply would have felt relieved that they let me go. When in the grips of mania, however, I acted as if it were my just due. I felt like a fucking celebrity.

When the Cadillac my father had given me died, I wasn't all that concerned. I went to a local car dealership and picked out a used vehicle. Money wasn't a problem; I just forged Dad's name on the loan application. It would have worked, too, had they not called him to confirm. When he told them he hadn't— and wouldn't—cosign for the car, I turned to the MRT, who was still working as a car salesman. When Grandma Jennie found out, she was furious at her brother. Didn't he know how sick I was? And besides, I couldn't afford it. My uncle sold me a car anyway, a brand-new Chevy Lumina.

In the MRT's defense, I was at my manic best; in other words able to sell snow to a snowman. Whenever he waivered I reminded him that if he didn't sell me a car, I would just get one at another dealership.

As part of the deal for the Lumina, I had to trade in the Cadillac. This meant delivering it to the MRT's dealership, about forty minutes from Grandma Jennie's house. Most people might think it was a problem that the car was not running; I, however, remained undeterred. I simply used my rental car to *push* the Cadillac the whole way with Ed Fradkin, one of my frat brothers, steering it. For months I had to hear his complaints of neck pain from my rear-ending the Caddy down the road.

The Lumina was sleek, fast, and perfectly suited to my purpose: constant motion. Even working two jobs didn't tire me; I couldn't sit still for a minute. The nursing home where I worked was about twenty miles south of Grandma Jennie's house. It took a half hour each way. Any sane person would have brought their lunch or grabbed a sandwich at a local deli. Not me. I sped home every day, often getting pulled over and even running out of gas a few times. One day I accidentally cut off two guys in a pickup truck then watched, adrenaline pumping, as they angrily gestured at me. They were pretty big guys, but that only made it more of a challenge. I motioned for them to pull over, preparing myself for a fight. I had no doubt that I could take them both on, but then I saw one of them step out of the truck armed with a crowbar. I debated getting my aluminum bat out of the trunk but decided I didn't have the time before he branded me. I settled instead for speeding away while pointing to my flexed bicep.

Normal Joe was nowhere to be found that summer, and I couldn't have been happier. I spent most of my time in Belmar racing other cars in the Lumina or racing friends on foot. Arm wrestling and beating guys twice my size, I had once again become Manic Joe, that alter ego who had first made an appearance in Acapulco, the one with the big mouth, the cocky swagger, and balls to back it up. I spent every dollar I could get my hands on, even betting one guy a hundred dollars that I could dunk a basketball. Despite my best efforts, I could barely touch the rim.

People began to notice that I was out of control. I didn't hide my condition—or the fact that I was experiencing a high—from my Belmar friends. At first everyone loved my obnoxious humor and my willingness to buy rounds of drinks. Then I was often late for my shifts and rarely fulfilled the cleaning duties of my job. Some days I just clocked in but didn't work my shift. My attitude was, "Why should I have to clean the place? It's all going to be mine one day anyway." I got my cousin Frank a job there, and I was soon punching in his time card when he wasn't there. I didn't care. As far as I was concerned, I was running the show.

When a nearby bar went up for sale, I told everybody I was buying it. I even met with the owner, who was asking for a few hundred thousand dollars for the place. Despite having zero net worth, I told him "no problem" and began hiring everyone I knew. I even asked some people if they wanted to be partners. When someone told me I had no chance of buying the bar, I'd fire them or, if I had offered them a managerial position, demote them to something more menial.

While my manic exploits at Bar A were for the most part harmless, they could have had much more serious consequences at my other job. The nursing home had originally hired me as an orderly, but when the owner learned I was a college graduate he made me recreational director. Against the home's rules, I began taking the old folks off grounds. One of them was an alcoholic from England. I took him to a local bar, where he downed a pint of beer in seconds. I took other patients to the batting cage, often letting them drive the Lumina. The patients kept telling me I was more fun than the last recreational director.

I figured I was doing less damage in my new position

than I had as an orderly. Part of that job had been to bathe the patients. There was even a checklist with each body part included. Well, I wasn't scrubbing anyone's balls. I began each shift by checking off the "wash genitalia" box on all my patients' checklists.

While Grandma Jennie didn't know the specifics of my life in Belmar, she did realize my condition was getting worse. It was difficult to know what to do, especially since I had no desire to rid myself of Manic Joe, so she decided the time had come to reunite me with Kevin. Since that phone call a while back, neither of us had made any attempt to see the other. Grandma Jennie knew Kevin was home for the summer, so she called him at Mom's and invited him over. She said nothing about my illness, my falling out with Dad and Rita, or the fact that I was living with her and Grandpa Frank. When Kevin arrived in Manalapan, Grandma Jennie told him, "Your brother Joe had a little falling out with your father. He's living here now."

She then further confused Kevin by completely changing the subject. "Look at the car my brother sold him," she said, pulling out a brochure for the Lumina.

When I pulled up to Grandma Jennie's and saw a Toyota Camry with New York plates and a "Think Snow" bumper sticker, I knew Kevin had arrived. He had been fascinated by weather, especially snow, since we were kids. Whenever it snowed, we could always find him by the window staring dreamily at the flakes.

Kevin greeted me at the door with a hug. Manic as all hell, I was afraid he would think I was on cocaine or something.

So I pulled him aside and, in five minutes, told him every-thing that had happened to me over the last two years.... Well, almost everything. I left out my physical relationship with Rita. I wasn't embarrassed; I'd had no problem telling Mike Miccio about it. But telling my brother was a completely dif-ferent story, and I realized I was hanging on to the last vestiges of loyalty to my father.

Kevin had no real knowledge of manic depression and, like most people who are unfamiliar with the illness, had no idea of its magnitude. It would be quite a while before he understood it meant more than I was happy one day, sad the next. He was, however, impressed with the pitted acne scars on my back, the result of my high lithium dosage.

"You gotta tell Mom," he said after we had spoken about it for a while.

Nodding, I picked up the phone. I hadn't seen her in nearly three years, and normally I would have been terribly nervous to call her, let alone to reveal some deep dark secret. Manic Joe, however, had no problem giving her the details of my illness.

Unlike Kevin, Mom realized immediately that I was pretty sick; she could tell from the medications. After I was done talking to her, Kevin got on the phone and suggested he stay with me for a couple of days. Mom agreed.

That afternoon I took Kevin with me to the nursing home. It would be the beginning of his eye-opening glimpse into the world of Manic Joe. The first person he met was my boss, Molly, who said she really liked me but wasn't going to be able to cover for me much longer. At Kevin's quizzical look, she glanced pointedly at the clock. I had just returned from a three-hour lunch break.

Next I introduced him to the orderlies. He was amazed by how many of them, most of whom were black, said, "I want to be rich. I don't want to be poor my whole life. So I'm following your brother." I had been telling them I was buying a bar and they could come in as partners. The poor bastards believed I was going places and they would be riding my coattails out of the ghetto.

In their defense they had no idea I was nuts. Poor and uneducated, all they saw was a good-looking, fast-talking, college-educated white guy who drove a brand-new sports car. I was learning how easy it is to convince people of just about anything, especially when they are down on their luck. I had no doubt I could have conned them out of their paychecks every week; hell, I could have told them I was God and they would have believed me. Instead of using my powers for evil, however, I often lent them money. In fact that afternoon with Kevin, I made him drive around with me in Lakewood looking for a *moulignon* orderly who owed me money. Manic Joe, it seemed, was also a bigot.

When I was unable to track the guy down, I quickly shifted gears, telling Kevin we were going to Rutgers. I kept asking him, "Do you want to get laid?" To which he responded, "What do you think?" Little did he know, he had a better chance of getting laid at a convent than at Rutgers that afternoon. For starters it was summer recess, and no one was around; and, if my experiences were any indication, it wouldn't have been so easy to get a girl anyway. Still, riding on fumes and delusions of grandeur, I dragged him to a few of my old hangouts. As expected the bars were deserted. No problem—I told Kevin I'd get him laid in Belmar that night. To that he responded, "I'd settle for Grandma Jennie's sauce."

We had been running around all day, laughing and talking about everything and nothing. I was having a great time, but telling Kevin about Rita was never far from my thoughts. On the ride back to our grandparents' house, Aerosmith's "Janie's Got a Gun" came on the radio. I saw this as an opening.

I threw Kevin a sideways glance. "Know what this song is about?"

When he said he didn't, I told him it was about a girl who was attempting to kill herself because her father had molested her.

Having no idea what I was alluding to, Kevin snorted. "Thanks for the pick-me-up."

We started laughing again, and the moment was lost.

At eight o'clock we walked into the house to find a ticked-off Grandma Jennie waiting for us. She had cooked all afternoon and thought we'd be back for dinner. Once she saw that we were okay, her anger turned to relief, and she proceeded to stuff Kevin with ten years' worth of her incredible food.

After we had eaten enough for five people, I was ready to head to Belmar. Grandma Jennie begged us to stay over at her house, but her pleas fell on deaf ears. I had promised to get my brother laid, and even manic I liked to think of myself as a guy who kept his word. We got to Bar A to find it as dead as

Rutgers. The only way Kevin was getting any action that night was if I paid Snaggletooth, the ratty toothless lady who lived around the corner. Kevin wasn't game. After driving around town and introducing him to some of my friends, I took him to the beach house.

It didn't take Kevin long to figure out why I often drove to Grandma Jennie's after work instead of sleeping in Belmar. The beach house was merely a bungalow, and it was a real shit hole. Twelve guys lived there, and not one of them lifted a finger to clean. Every room was littered with trash and half-eaten plates of food, there was no air-conditioning, and the entire place reeked of garbage and mildew. It also had bedbugs. After what was probably the worst night of Kevin's life, I woke him at seven. I had to be at work at the nursing home by nine, and I wanted him to drive me back to Grandma Jennie's so I could shower for work.

Kevin and I hadn't spent that much time together since I had gone on my infamous "taxicab" ride in 1978, and even our rare visits had been marked by anxiety. In a lot of ways it was as if we had never been apart—at least that was how I felt. If he was shocked by Manic Joe's behavior he didn't say, even when I got in the passenger seat of the Lumina dressed in only my shoes and underwear. On the way to Manalapan, he missed a turn, nearly plowing into the back of a pickup truck. I didn't have my seatbelt on, and we laughed about how I would have looked flying out of the front seat, practically naked, onto the flatbed.

He was surprised, though, when conservative Grandma

Jennie had no reaction to my appearance. We had left her the night before cleaning up after the feast; when we returned the next morning, she was back in the kitchen frying up a dozen eggs for us. For the first time in years, we were eating together in her house, and she was going to enjoy every minute of it even if I was wearing what she called my "bloomers." I often drove that way to her house from Belmar, and, in her opinion, this was the least objectionable of my manic hijinks.

By that time Kevin was thoroughly exhausted. He had shown up at Grandma Jennie's the previous day expecting to hang out with his big brother; he had not expected twenty-four hours of the Manic Joe show. Instead of staying for a few days, he headed back to Merrick later that morning. I told him I'd be in Merrick the following week for his birthday on July 8. As it turned out, he wasn't the only one who was tired of me. That afternoon Molly finally fired me from the nursing home.

Although Kevin didn't get laid, didn't sleep, and nearly killed us driving the Lumina, our reunion was a triumphant one. With our father out of the picture, we were finally able to rebuild the close bond we'd had as kids. Now the only thing between us was Manic Joe. As promised I did make it to Merrick the following week, but I didn't get there in time to celebrate Kevin's birthday. Instead my mother, Beave, and Kevin awoke to the sound of their doorbell at 2:00 a.m. I don't know what shocked Mom more when she answered the door—the site of her estranged, manic son or the two strangers he had with him.

I had used my manic charm to convince Lou and Fat Ara—coworkers from Bar A—to take the two-hour drive to

Merrick with me. Lou was an easy sell; he was a nice guy who was working to pay for St. John's, where he was studying engineering. I had been deriding him the whole summer, telling him he was too dumb to be an engineer. Unfazed by my abuse, at the end of the summer he would thank me for giving him the time of his life. Like many people in Belmar, Lou enjoyed Manic Joe's exploits, particularly since they usually included buying everyone drinks.

Ara, a fat, miserable bastard, was harder to convince. Between his looks and his disposition, Ara couldn't get laid in a whorehouse with a C-note hanging out of each pocket. I'd promised him we'd take Beave's boat out to a bar on the water where even he would get some action.

By the time we got out to Merrick, it was too late to go out. My bleary-eyed mother began making up beds for the three of us, but Fat Ara insisted we go back home. By the time we left to go back to Jersey, it was four in the morning. Lou and Ara were furious with me, but as is always the case when I am manic, I couldn't have cared less. I hadn't slept in nearly thirty-six hours and knew I was finally about to crash. I handed Lou the keys and fell asleep as soon as we hit the Parkway. I later found out that to get back at me, they considered driving the car all the way to Washington, DC, and taking a train home. Eventually they saw the stupidity of their plan; basically I wouldn't have cared, and they would have been left buying the train tickets.

Before leaving Merrick I had promised Mom and Kevin I'd come back soon and at a more reasonable hour. Later in the week, I met them at Grandma Dar's in Canarsie. Grandma Dar made my favorite dish, linguini and white clam sauce, and I showed Grandpa Jack the engine in my Lumina. They couldn't help but notice I was very different from the quiet young man they had seen three years earlier. I was fidgety and talking a lot of nonsense. I repeatedly told Grandma Dar I was going to take the whole family on vacation, which wouldn't have been so bad except I also insisted the DeBlasis would be there as well. This had always been a fantasy of mine—us all being a family again—but it was only in a manic state that I gave voice to it.

I made it up to Long Island one more time that summer. Our uncle Jimmy had gotten Kevin a summer job in Long Beach as a security guard in an apartment complex. When I arrived at Townhouse Apartments, I found Kevin driving around in one of those security golf carts. Still a manic mess, I kept asking to race the cart. "Grandma Jennie could outrun this thing," responded Kevin with a grin. I then said he should get out of the cart so I could race him on foot. Kevin had been a track star and an excellent base runner. I had always been rather slow, but as Manic Joe I was convinced not only that I could outrun my younger brother but that I was fast enough to play professional baseball.

After Kevin finished his shift, we headed over to the beach to hang out with his best friend, Mike DeBonis. Mike had gone to high school with Kevin and was now catching for a college baseball team. The three of us were throwing a ball around and it got by me. To demonstrate my foot speed to Kevin and Mike, I took off after it at what I thought was breakneck speed.

According to Kevin I was some sight—all 225 pounds of me hauling ass across the packed beach, weaving between blankets and startled sun worshippers. I was kicking up sand all over the place and pissing off a lot of people in the process. Mike was laughing hysterically; Kevin, however, realized this was no joke. I was serious about my speed and my plan to play in the majors. While my antics elicited a deep belly laugh from Mike, Kevin's stomach sank. It was at that moment he finally realized the gravity of my illness.

CHAPTER 15

Broken and Reconnected

As the expression goes, what goes up must come down. As the summer of 1991 drew to a close, so did my high. Suddenly I felt the pressure of meeting my exorbitant car payment as well as the fact that my life was completely without direction. I don't know if this caused the depression or was the result of it—it's often a "chicken or the egg" situation. Sometimes there is no external reason for sinking into a depression; it's just the chemical imbalance in the brain. Whatever the reason there was little doubt that by late August, I was falling into the abyss once again. On what would be my last night at Bar A, I felt a terrible desperation. For the first time in my life, I stole like a bandit, grabbing handfuls of cash from the register and tip jar. The next morning I gave Grandma Jennie $400, mostly singles, so she could write a check for the car payment. By afternoon I was suicidal.

Brokenhearted by my condition, Grandma Jennie wasted no time in having me admit myself to Staten Island Hospital. She wanted to ensure my safety; she was also hoping the situation would bring my father around. This was despite the fact that he had ignored her repeated pleas over the summer to reconnect with me. He had made it clear he wanted nothing to do with me.

Like Grandma Jennie I hadn't made it easy for him to forget me. I had showed up at his office a few times that summer. Our conversations started out civilly enough but quickly deteriorated into shouting matches when I brought up my physical relationship with Rita. The mania, coupled with the distance from my father, had given me the guts to push the issue. I insisted Rita was a pedophile and even suggested to him that her father probably molested her when she was little. Although I had absolutely no proof, I speculated that Amerigo used to come up from his wine cellar drunk and fondle her. Some of my therapists had speculated about this as well. Apparently it is very common for a person who was molested as a child to become an abuser.

When I suggested this to Dad, he claimed to have asked Rita if anything like that had ever happened. He said she denied it. As if I were going to believe her. Even if she had been molested, I doubted she'd tell my father; after all it would only make her more culpable for our physical relationship.

The bottom line was that Dad was sticking to his guns and with his second wife. He stopped taking Grandma Jennie's calls. During one of her visits to see me in the hospital, Dr. Adler told her, "Your son has his head buried in the sand. If he pulls it out, he won't know whether to shoot himself or his wife." Finally she had to admit defeat—my father was not coming back into my life. That was when she called Mom.

Although I had seen my mother twice over the past few months, we hadn't made any serious inroads on bridging the thirteen-year gap in our relationship. On those two occasions, I was manic and far too wired to sit down and have a serious conversation about all that had occurred. In that state it would have been impossible to sort through the years of guilt, not to mention all the lies my father had told me about her. It wasn't any easier to discuss these issues while depressed, but thanks to Grandma Jennie and my new therapist, Carol Davis, that was what happened.

Carol, who had taken over my case from Thomas DiMartini, was aware of my past with Rita. Like DiMartini she stressed to me that the situation was not my fault. She also pointed out that it was unnatural for my father to prohibit me and my brothers from dating. Growing boys had certain physical needs, and while Stephen had snuck out to meet girls his age, I had remained under my father's thumb and under Rita's nose. Carol made it clear that she thought Rita's behavior was criminal and, normally, an offense requiring mandatory reporting. She suspected that Dad's influence at the hospital was the only reason it hadn't been reported back in 1989. Realizing that little could be done to fix the past or repair my relationship with my father, Carol focused instead on my mother.

I cannot imagine what Mom was feeling during that time. Ever since the day I had disappeared from her house at the age of nine, she had dreamed of reestablishing a relationship with me. Now that dream had turned into a nightmare. I was no longer the happy child who had played Mean Joe Green in Mr. Vecchio's house; I was a full-grown man, essentially a stranger, and in a mental ward on suicide watch. None of that mattered to her. I was still her little boy, and she was going to be there for me.

She started visiting me every day after work. She was actually working two jobs—as the director of Mercy Medical Center's School of Radiography and as an adjunct professor at CW Post teaching radiation physics. Both these positions were near her house on Long Island, and every evening she'd brave the Belt Parkway during rush hour to see me on Staten Island. It didn't matter that I was so depressed I hardly spoke to her. On the way she would stop and pick me up something for dinner. I was happy to see her and grateful for the food, but that still didn't keep me from wanting to die.

One day she showed up with Aunt Paula, who hadn't seen me since Mom's wedding nearly ten years earlier. Completely devastated by my condition, Paula sobbed the whole time. Mom never cried, though, at least not in front of me. She had survived the hell of my father's defection, the breakup of her marriage, and the loss of two sons. She had learned to make the best of a miserable situation if only for Kevin's sake. She did the same thing now for mine. She began to discuss with Carol the prospect of having me live with her and Beave when I was discharged. When she consulted Kevin, he was floored. Like Mom he had prayed for a reunion, but given my father's smear campaign he'd never thought it possible that I (or Stephen) would ever live with them again.

Shocked or not, Kevin also rallied to my side, driving up from UPenn to visit every Saturday from mid-September until my discharge in late November. He too would stop and pick up food for me on the way. Oftentimes he would visit me for lunch then head to Grandma Dar's for dinner. He would then pass back through Staten Island on his way to Philadelphia, dropping off whatever delicious meal she had made. Whether she made shrimp scampi or linguini and white clam sauce, I was the best-fed nut in the place.

Unfortunately once manic depression manifests, it is not affected by things like familial love and support. Despite the efforts of Mom, Kevin, and both sets of grandparents, I remained horribly depressed throughout that fall. I slept most of the time and spent every waking moment thinking about how I could die. When I got tired of coming up with ways to kill myself, I envisioned elaborate scenarios in which I would die by "accident." The meds didn't help, and neither did the light therapy Dr. Adler prescribed. Originally used for people suffering from seasonal affective disorder (depression during the winter months due to reduced sunlight), doctors had also had some success in using light therapy for non-seasonal depression. I didn't know whether it was helping anyone else, but it did nothing for me.

Every morning at six o'clock, the hospital staff woke me.

They would sit me in front of a bright fluorescent light and have me stare into it for an hour. Some days they left me alone so they could tend to other patients. This was my cue to go back to sleep. I figured I had enough to deal with without this torture. When I finally summoned the energy to confront Dr. Adler about it, he confessed that it probably wouldn't elevate my mood. He had continued to wake me early because he felt I was becoming too comfortable at the hospital.

The truth was Dr. Adler had to be careful about the strength of the light he used as well as the length of the sessions. While light therapy may be helpful with normal depression, it holds a particular risk for those suffering from bipolar. If the patient is exposed to too much light or for too long, it can trigger mania.

When after three months my depression still hadn't lifted, Dr. Adler mentioned the possibility of administering electric shock therapy. I had never felt worse in my life, but I still refused. To me this was something that was done to crazy people. I might have wanted to die, but I certainly didn't want to be sitting in a chair with drool running down my chin. This was the public perception of this treatment—and, like everyone else, I bought in to it.

As November approached, Carol Davis decided it was time for Mom to sit in on one of my therapy sessions. Although I didn't say a lot during her daily visits, they had done much to melt the distance between us. Just by showing up, sitting with me, and bringing food, she had reminded me of what a loving, caring mother she was. She had doted on me when I was a child, and nothing—not my father's manipulation or even my illness—had changed how she felt about me. I was starting to feel close to her again, and maybe that was why I still hadn't told her about my relationship with Rita. Would she judge me for it? I had no idea, and I didn't want to find out. Besides, it was over, so what was the point? Then again I didn't think there was much point to anything.

The point, Carol argued, was that it would further strengthen my support system if Mom knew the full extent of what had gone on during my years away from her, particularly since it might have contributed to my illness. Depressed and exhausted, I eventually gave in. On the day of the session, I didn't even have the energy to be nervous. In a monotone voice that lacked all trace of emotion, I went through the whole affair with Rita from our first kiss on the lips to the last time we fooled around when I was home from Rutgers. Most of that session is a blur, but I will never forget Mom's face as I spoke: it went from complete shock to white-hot rage; at one point I even thought she was going to be sick.

My mom had read enough about bipolar to know it has a genetic component. However, after I was done telling my story, Carol explained that while genetics do play a role, bipolar can also be triggered by trauma. She believed that my childhood experiences, including the "taxi ride" to Staten Island, being coerced into telling lies about Mom, and Rita's behavior, had all created a perfect storm that contributed to my disease.

Mom drove back to Merrick that night, her head teeming with everything Carol and I had told her. She thought about all she had been through over those many years when she thought

I preferred my father to her. Of course she was devastated to learn not only that her son had been molested but that it might have triggered a debilitating mental illness. At the same time, she couldn't help but notice the irony of the situation. My father had screwed around on her with half of Maimonides, then dumped her so he could be free to resume the life of a bachelor. When that wasn't enough, he had brainwashed her children against her. Then, after finally finding the woman he wanted to spend the rest of his life wife with—the woman he had chosen over his own family—she started fooling around with his oldest son. I couldn't fault Mom for thinking that after all he had put her and everyone else through, he had finally gotten his just desserts. The fact that he refused to acknowledge Rita's betrayal only made it more pathetic. It also made Mom all the more thankful that she had found a man like Beave.

Even through the fog of my depression, I was especially moved when Beave came to visit me at the hospital. I had met him only a few times, but he showed me the same love and support one shows their own kids. Beave had always been a natural-born father. He and his first wife had adopted two girls, Sherie and Beth; they also lived in Merrick, with their mother. Since the early 1980s, Beave had been raising Kevin as if he were his biological son. While Kevin had never called him Dad, he had given him the endearing nickname. Now he offered to "adopt" me as well.

"I have been Kevin's father for nearly ten years," he said as he sat by my hospital bed. "If you want to, come live with us and I will be your father too."

I nodded, amazed that after everything I had been through

I was getting another chance at a family, with a whole new set of parents who actually had my best interests at heart. I had also gotten my brother Kevin back, which I considered a miracle after being torn apart at such a young age. The best part was he could always make me smile no matter how down I was. When he found out about my relationship with my stepmother, he quipped, "Had I known about what would go on with Rita, I would have jumped in the cab with you." Kevin's remark earned him a murderous look from Mom, but I couldn't suppress a laugh.

Gradually my mood did begin to lift, although I didn't know whether it was the meds, the therapy, or just the whims of my brain chemistry. Dr. Adler wasn't sure either, but he decided I was ready to be released. The day before Thanksgiving, Mom and Beave came to get me and bring me back to Merrick, no doubt thinking it would be a new beginning. It was a new beginning all right, just not the kind they were expecting. A week later I was cycling toward full-blown mania, and the peaceful existence they had known was over.

It is hard to know what will trigger a so-called bipolar event. The triggers range from seasonal changes to the pressures of a lousy job. Basically life events that most people would take in stride can send someone like me cycling in one direction or another. One of the most common triggers is travel; another is changing residences. I had had my first mania while in Acapulco, another when I moved to Grandma Jennie's, and now after moving to Merrick. But was that the real reason or merely a coincidence? Each manic period had also come after a horrible depression, so there was no way of knowing whether it was life circumstances or simple biology. Either way, less than a month after Beave issued his heartfelt offer he was probably wondering what he had gotten himself into. I'm sure he wondered that every day of the next three years as I swung between depression and mania then back again, often with only a few weeks of stability in between.

Two weeks after I relocated to Merrick, Mom and Beave were placing frantic calls to Dr Adler. They had seen me manic during the previous summer. But those had been brief visits; now they had me 24/7. I was completely out of control, ranting and raving at all hours of the day and night, and they didn't have the slightest idea how to handle it. Kevin was at school, so they didn't even have him to lean on. Other than putting me back in the hospital, Adler was their only hope.

When he heard that I did not yet have a new psychiatrist, he told them to bring me to his home in nearby Oceanside, Long Island. This was risky and highly unusual, but after witnessing my drama with Dad and Rita, Adler had taken pity on me and my family. That night he prescribed more mood stabilizers and some tranquilizers; he also gave Mom and Beave recommendations for Long Island shrinks. As we said good-bye to Dr. Adler, we had no idea he was figuring I wouldn't survive too much longer. When I finally saw him again twenty-one years later, he would admit as much: "Joe, you must have an incredible will to live."

I almost said, "Depends on the day." Instead I shrugged and muttered, "I guess."

It was only a ten-minute ride from Dr. Adler's back to

Merrick, but to Mom and Beave it must have felt like hours. We were travelling eastbound on Merrick Road when I started screaming at them to let me off at the side of the road. "I got to find a girl to get laid!"

When Kevin returned home for Christmas break, he was looking forward to a rest from the all-nighters and the lousy college diet. Instead he found that Manic Joe had returned. My mother was visibly exhausted from trying to go to work, take care of the house, and deal with me. Beave, on the other hand, was holding it together. He would continue to do so for the next decade. Even when the rest of the family was in hysterics over my increasingly bizarre behavior, Beave was our rock. I honestly don't know what my mother would have done without him.

Manic Joe was back with a vengeance, and he certainly didn't care about how his behavior affected everyone else. One day I took an entire bottle of Klonopin, a powerful tranquilizer. I did not want to kill myself; I was simply in a foul mood and wanted to scare everyone. Mission accomplished. Mom raced to the phone and called Mercy's ER, and the staffer on the other end told her I could die if I did not get my stomach pumped immediately.

Beave had just walked in the front door after a long day of teaching followed by a buying expedition for his weekend sweater business. As Mom and Kevin frantically explained the situation, I stood there pleased with the stir I had caused. Despite what that fool at the hospital said, I *knew* I wasn't going to die.

Cool as a cucumber, Beave said he'd drive us to Mercy as soon as he'd removed the several dozen sweaters from the backseat of his car. He had heard from Mom that there had been smash-and-grabs in Mercy's parking lots, and he wasn't taking any unnecessary chances. That was just like Beave, calmly calculating that the few extra minutes wouldn't kill me. He was right. I did not even need my stomach pumped. I did, however, have to drink a solution that looked like charcoal and tasted like shit. Even manic I knew I deserved it.

Kevin, however, did not deserve it. For years he had dreamed of the day when he would be sleeping under the same roof with one of his brothers. If there were ever a time when the saying "be careful what you wish for was appropriate, this was it. I wasn't a dream; I was a nightmare. For some reason, which made complete sense to me at the time, I purchased a briefcase and insisted on carrying it everywhere. I filled it with everything from my Brut cologne to my wallet. It had snaps that made a loud crackling noise every time I opened or closed it, which I did incessantly.

"That noise could wake the dead," Kevin growled one night when I woke him from yet another sound sleep. That was his mistake. From then on I opened it even more often, sometimes to retrieve something I needed but often just to annoy him. I carried that briefcase around so much that Kevin started referring to me as Joseph Wharton, founder of UPenn's esteemed business school.

Kevin's other goal over the break was to research law schools as he planned on applying for the following fall. I didn't let him do that. As he sat at his computer, I'd stand over him and ask magnanimously, "Do you want me to get you in to Harvard?"

To someone unfamiliar with bipolar disorder, this might seem like a benign albeit ridiculous question. By then, however, Kevin knew enough to answer in a way that would not agitate me.

"How are you going to get me in to Harvard?" His tone was light, his eyes still on the screen.

"What do you know?" I exploded, hands wildly gesturing like an old Italian, "You don't think I can get you in to Harvard?"

This got Kevin's attention. He looked up at me and saw that being rational—or humorous—wasn't an option. He smiled sheepishly and held up his hands. "Yeah, yeah, Joe. I know you're going to get me in."

This only enraged me more. "Are you just jerking me off? Don't jerk me off just to placate me."

Realizing he couldn't win, he apologized and continued counting the minutes until he could return to UPenn. But he still had one more week on Long Island and one more very important holiday: our first New Year's Eve together since Shangri-La. I was determined that we would have a blast. When we asked Kevin's friend Mike DeBonis to go out with us, he said he couldn't—he was broke. Beave wouldn't hear of it and gave him some pocket money. We originally planned to drive down to Bar A but gave up on that idea when we thought about the Jersey traffic we'd be stuck in all night. Instead we ended up at a club in West Hempstead, Long Island.

It wasn't until we got there that Kevin and I realized we were wearing matching paisley dress shirts. Aunt Paula had given them to us for Christmas. Mine was red and Kevin's was green, but they matched in every other way. A dark club, New Year's Eve, who would notice? The DJ, for one, who couldn't resist announcing to the crowd, "Everybody is here tonight! We even have the Paisley Brothers in the house." Everyone who was not yet totally inebriated—including Mike DeBonis—laughed hysterically at this quick-witted record spinner. Embarrassed and feeling stupid in the matching hideous shirts, I blamed Kevin for our fashion faux pas. With the night ruined, we left shortly after the ball dropped.

Drunk and pissed off, I continued to berate him on the car ride home. Kevin, who was a little drunk himself and exhausted from dealing with my obnoxious behavior for weeks on end, finally reached his breaking point.

"You guys fucking left me with Mom," he screamed as soon as we pulled up at the house. "You left me alone to rot. Now you come back into my life, and you're treating me like shit. Fuck you."

He looked like he was about to cry, but at that moment I couldn't have cared less. There it was, New Year's Eve, and instead of having fun he was dredging up the past.

"Kevin, I was fucking nine years old. What did you want me to do?"

"You weren't nine the whole time. You could have driven out to see me or even called when you were out of the house."

That dose of reality was stronger than any meds I'd been

taking. Kevin was right. I'd had plenty of opportunities to reach out over the years. I had been so under my father's spell, it had never crossed my mind to contact Kevin, Mom, or even Grandma Dar and Grandpa Jack. Now that we were adults, it seemed like a woefully inadequate explanation, and for the first time I truly understood how hurt Kevin had been when I, then Stephen, disappeared from his life.

I might have understood it, but I did not handle it very well. Trying to have a serious conversation with me when I'm manic is as futile as shouting into the wind. If I had been agitated before, I now became like a lunatic.

"Do you want me to kill myself?" Without waiting for an answer, I ran into the house and headed to the kitchen to get a knife. Kevin and Mike ran in after me. "If it makes you feel better, I will kill myself right here!"

Kevin ran upstairs to wake Mom and Beave, then retreated to his bedroom, where he sobbed uncontrollably. He had finally expressed how he had felt all those years only to have me freak out on him. The fact that I was sick didn't make it any easier for him to deal with.

Luckily I wasn't serious about killing myself, but I was out of control. As unfazed as ever, Beave walked into the kitchen and bravely faced me. I was so crazed, I barely remember what he said to me; all I remember is his gentle tone. Eventually he managed to calm me down.

Then he went to deal with Mike DeBonis, who had been in the living room the whole time. He was a little drunk as well and crying like a baby. Apparently, as close as he and Kevin were, this was the first time he had heard how horrible it had been for Kevin to be so close with his brothers as children only to have them both desert him. Mike had always sensed sadness in Kevin, and now he had witnessed its root.

After that blowup things got better between Kevin and me. It wouldn't always be easy, but at least he had gotten some things off his chest. Besides, we had something else to look forward to: our half brother Frank's basketball game later that week. Frank was a star on the team at his high school, Christian Brothers Academy in Holmdel.

Before I got sick, I used to go to all his games. Frank was an excellent shooting guard, known for being able to light it up from all over. Even more exciting than watching him was watching Dad. From the way he screamed like a lunatic at the refs, the opposing team's coaches, and anyone else who rubbed him the wrong way, people might have thought *he* was manic. Nothing else mattered when Frank had a game, least of all the waiting room full of patients who were wondering why it took three hours to get in to have their throat culture or prostate exam. On game days Dad would rush out of the office telling his staff he'd be back soon, then he'd return hours later and resume appointments as though he had never left.

Grandma Jennie and Grandpa Frank had never missed a game either, even after my father ordered them to stop coming. My father had used his sons to punish them before, and he had no problem doing it again. In his mind their decision to take me in meant they forfeited the rights to see Frank and Matthew. Like she had done before, Grandma Jennie ignored him until the day Dad arrived at a game and witnessed a shouting match between his parents and Rita. When she told them, "I don't want you two to have the pleasure of seeing your grandson play," Grandpa Frank responded with his usual mantra, calling Rita "a second-hand piece of shit." This time he added, "And you're a goddamn pedophile."

Later that night my father called Grandma Jennie. After his usual "you disrespect my wife, you disrespect me" and "in my house he was disrespecting my wife," Dad got down to business. If his mother wouldn't follow his order to stay away from Frank's games, he'd just have to use his trump card: Grandpa Frank's felony drug-trafficking conviction.

"If I see either of you at another game, I am going to report to Christian Brothers that Dad is a convicted drug dealer. He will be cuffed, and you will be escorted off the school grounds. Stay away from me, my wife, and our children. You made your bed. You love your other grandchildren more than me. This is what you get. Don't even call me at the office. You are dead to me."

After blasting my grandfather once again for his weed escapade, Grandma Jennie was forced to admit she had lost this particular battle. They never saw another of Frank's games; in fact they never saw either of my half brothers again.

As for me, going to Frank's games had essentially ended with my first depression back in 1988. Shortly after I was admitted to Staten Island Hospital the following spring, Frank had dedicated his game to me. Right before they began play, in the middle of the team huddle, he announced that his older brother Joe was in the hospital suffering from severe mania. He then poured in fifty points in my honor. I have often wondered what my father thought of that announcement considering he never wanted anyone to know about my illness; regardless, I was incredibly moved by what Frank had done.

A lot had gone on since that day, not the least of which was Kevin's successful lawsuit against Dad. We were the last people Dad wanted to see at Frank's game that January, but he could not stop us from coming like he did with my grandparents. I had yet to have an arrest record, Kevin was a squeaky-clean student, and he was chomping at the bit to confront our father.

Kevin is usually one of the least aggressive people I've ever met; in fact, during one of my manic rants, I told him he shares a testicle with Stephen. But that day, as we headed to the game, he was a completely different person. For the first time in years, he was going to come face to face with the man who had taken his oldest brother away then returned him a broken, bipolar lunatic. Not to mention that he had devastated our mother and caused both sets of grandparents a world of heartache. Fueled by a lifetime of anger, Kevin was so jumpy he made *me* nervous. I wondered how this was all going to go down.

It didn't take long to find out. Shortly after entering Christian Brothers, we ran into Dad in an otherwise empty corridor. Kevin wasted no time. He marched right up to our father and said, "You'd better go find your wife. I hear one of the JV players is missing."

I had never seen that expression on my brother's face before—it was pure, barely controlled rage.

It took a minute, but I knew exactly when the comment registered with Dad. A slow, hot flush crept over his face as he stared down at Kevin. "You know what you are?" he snarled, his teeth clenched. "You're the fuckin' hole in the scumbag."

Referring to the successful lawsuit for his college tuition, Kevin snapped back, "I'm the *sixty-thousand-dollar* hole, you stupid, fat, fucking pussy-whipped bastard. While you were working your nuts off sixteen hours a day, your wife was home grabbing Joe's. They christened every room in the mansion you built them."

Dad rushed at Kevin, but before he could get at him I interceded, grabbing Dad by his jacket and throwing all three hundred pounds of him up against the wall.

My father was beet-red and panting like an animal as he strained against me. "Joey, get your hands off me. Get your damn hands off me, Joey."

"Yeah? What are you going to do about it, fat man? What are you going to do?"

I don't know what would have happened if some people hadn't spilled out from the gymnasium and caught sight of us. The moment was broken, and we went our separate ways.

After leaving the school, Kevin and I headed to Grandma Jennie's for sauce. Proud of what he had said to our father, Kevin recounted every word of the venomous exchange. In his mind he had taken some small measure of revenge not only for himself but for me, Mom, and our grandparents. Grandma Jennie and Grandpa Frank listened quietly, but they were no doubt sick to their stomachs to hear what had become of our once-happy family. As for me, my back hurt for days after hurling my father against the wall, but it was well worth it.

Around that time I started seeing Dr. Louis K. Teitelbaum, the kind, caring man who would be my primary psychiatrist for the next twenty years. He once told me I was his longest-running patient. This surprised me at first; then I realized two things. The first was that he had probably lost many patients to suicide; the second was that many chronically ill psychiatric patients move on to new doctors every few years, hoping to get different results. Unfortunately, with diseases like manic depression, management of symptoms is the best you're going to get no matter what shrink you go to. I saw other doctors during that time—whatever hospital the police or my family had me committed to had a psychiatrist on staff who would then consult with Dr. Teitelbaum. For better or worse, we were stuck with each other.

Not only did he always accept my family's anxiety-ridden, late-night calls, but he also stood up to the countless unscrupulous luxury-car salesmen who thought they would take advantage of my manic state. "No, Joe cannot afford the nine-hundred-dollar monthly car payment. He is a manic depressive and only collects five hundred dollars a month from the government."

He also stood up to me. No matter how agitated or threatening I was, he would ask me in his soothe, calming voice to calm down. His reaction to my escapades was always the same: never shocked, never startled, always matter-of-fact. In that way he was just like Beave.

One time I was trying to convince Dr. Teitelbaum that I wasn't that manic so he wouldn't commit me to Mercy. He asked me to recount my day.

"Woke up, went to the gym then the Marybill Diner. Then my brother Kevin and I went to a brothel."

Next to me was a very embarrassed Kevin, who quickly exclaimed, "It was a Korean massage parlor, and I didn't go for the tug. I have a political career to think about." The two of us broke into hysterical laughter.

Dr. Teitelbaum did not find us amusing. With his typical stoicism, he scribbled some notes, never cracking a smile. After a few moments, he looked up at my brother. "Do *you* think Joseph needs to be hospitalized?"

After years of cycling between mania and depression, I eventually had to admit to myself that my current course of treatment was not working. The meds were woefully inefficient in controlling my moods, and the outpatient group-therapy program I was attending was a joke. I was unable able to hold down a job, had no money, and had started receiving Medicaid benefits. Clearly something else had to be done to try to break the cycle, and Dr. Teitelbaum believed electroconvulsive therapy—also known as electroshock therapy or ECT—was that something.

Electroshock therapy has been utilized in one form or another since the 1930s. While the specific methods have changed over the years, the basic premise has not: the electric impulses induce seizures that cause changes in the brain, literally jolting it out of depression. Despite a massive body of research, scientists still do not completely understand how this happens, but for people who do not respond well to meds, it is arguably the most effective treatment out there.

Historically ECT was considered barbaric, and some in the field still feel that way. However, the use of general anesthesia along with changes in the placement of the electrodes has done much to mitigate negative side effects. The patient feels nothing during the procedure because he or she is asleep.

When Dr. Adler had suggested ECT a few years earlier, I had refused to consider it. Like many people I saw ECT as a form of torture that destroyed the mind and turned you into some shadow of your former self, if not a complete vegetable. After several hospitalizations in 1991 and 1992 for both mania and severe depression with suicidal ideation, however, I began to listen. I couldn't take the constant cycling anymore, and neither could my family; we were all exhausted. The only break they got was when I was in the hospital, but we all knew the nightmare would begin again as soon as I got out. The standard for being released from Mercy Hospital was "stability" as determined by medical staff. Essentially this meant I was eating two meals a day, was sleeping six to eight hours a night (instead of around the clock or not at all), and wasn't fantasizing about jumping off buildings. This was the best that high doses of lithium, Depakote, and other meds could do. But that stability was tenuous, to say the least, and no one, including me, knew when I would start spiraling again or in which direction. I finally consented to ECT in the summer of 1992.

I received my first treatment when hospitalized at Mercy that July, then continued them on an outpatient basis. I was often suicidal when I arrived early in the morning. I'd have the treatment, and, like magic, the depression would begin to lift usually by that afternoon. Sometimes I'd even be out that same night, partying with Kevin at a local bar. It was the closest thing to a miracle I have ever experienced. I usually had short-term memory loss, sometimes even forgetting that I had been there at all. In fact many experts claim this as part of the reason ECT is so successful in treating depressives—it makes them forget the circumstances that made them depressed in the first place. While it didn't make me forget my turbulent childhood, it often erased the event that had triggered my most recent descent into hopelessness. I only had one bad experience when my mouth guard moved during the procedure and I almost bit through my tongue. In any event the ECT was never the gruesome experience people usually envision.

The greatest risk is the general anesthesia, but as I see it, the people getting ECT are so depressed that they want to die anyway. What have they got to lose? They have a much better chance of killing themselves while they wait for the latest antidepressant to kick in than dying during the procedure. Although I had never seriously attempted to take my own life, the temptation—and therefore the risk—was always there.

While ECT spared me untold months of mental anguish, it certainly was not a cure for my illness. I heard that some people received ECT treatments for their mania as well; others got "maintenance" ECT meaning the electroshocks were administered when they were neither manic nor depressed in an effort to prevent the mood swings. I quickly decided these options were not for me. The last thing I wanted when I was high was for someone to bring me down; I wasn't really interested in preventing my manias either, for it was only during those periods that I experienced any sense of freedom. And, as it turned out, the ECT was so effective at pulling me out of my depression that it would often send me into full-flown mania. This was great for me in the moment; on the other hand, it was often the consequences of my manic behavior—for example getting into debt—that would lead to the next depression. In other words it became a different kind of cycle. For this reason I would eventually stop the ECT altogether. I was already walking a constant tightrope between my mood swings; it didn't make much sense to continue a treatment that was exacerbating it. However, by that time, Dr. Teitelbaum had administered scores of ECT treatments.

CHAPTER 16

Say What?!

By late fall 1992, I felt well enough to hold down a job. The ECT had brought me some measure of stability; the depression was gone, and I was only slightly up, meaning I was cheerful and charismatic without the irresponsibility of full-blown mania. Given my temperament and a background in finance, sales seemed like a good fit.

I was hired as a financial planner by the Equitable Life Assurance Agency, a collection of individually run agencies that provided retirement and investment products to individuals and companies. Part of my job at the Green Agency was to secure new clients, and I would receive commissions on the business I brought in. Like all new hires, I would be on probation for a while to see if I could produce. At first everything seemed to be going well; I invested $500 in mass mailings, made endless cold calls, and was soon generating a fair amount of sales leads.

Other than helping Beave at the flea markets, I hadn't had a job with any real responsibility in a long time, and it felt good to be part of the world again. But as is often the case when I get a new job or make any lifestyle changes, I soon began to feel that familiar downward pull: hopelessness coupled with a lack of desire to work or do anything else, for that matter. I had been around this block enough to know where it led.

I called my immediate supervisor, and told him I was quitting. I did not elaborate as to why; I just said that selling life insurance was not for me. Then it was back to the hospital for more ECT. When in February the depression began to lift, I called my former supervisor, took a deep breath, and told him the real reason I had left. It was the first time I had revealed the full extent of my condition to someone who wasn't either a family member or a physician.

I wasn't sure what to expect, but he seemed to take it in stride; he even spoke to Mr. Green, the managing agent, on my behalf. They agreed to hire me back, but I would still have to complete the probationary period. That was fine with me—I was just happy to be given a second chance and relieved to be working with people who, presumably, would understand if I needed treatment in the future.

At first I didn't understand why business was so slow; I had been doing quite well before the depression hit. Then I found out that my "understanding" boss was diverting leads from my original mass mailing to his brother, who had been hired while I was out. Together they were effectively hijacking my potential clients—and commissions—after I had done all the legwork.

This was one of one of those times when I truly appreciated my mania. If I had been depressed or even at baseline, I would have tucked my tail between my legs and ignored what they were doing. Still slightly up, however, I called my supervisor again, this time to tell him what I thought of him and what he could do with the leads. By the end of the conversation, we agreed I should move on.

While I was angry about what had happened, I wasn't all that concerned; after all I wasn't the first guy to be screwed over by a coworker. I would just move to another agency and resume my work. Unfortunately I was about to find out that the rules are different when the victim of such behavior has manic depression—or any other illness, for that matter.

A few days later, I went in for an interview with Mike Rosenthal, an Equitable district manager with the Schulman Agency. It went very well; I came across as pleasant and motivated, and Mr. Rosenthal was impressed by my previous work.

"Everything's fine," he told me as we prepared to wrap it up. "I just need to speak with Mr. Green before we make it official." He then told me to come back the next day so we could finalize things. I left his office feeling confident that while perhaps I had been unfairly treated at the Green Agency, it would all work out in the end. When I returned the next morning, Rosenthal greeted me warmly, still behaving as if I were already part of the team. Then the phone rang, and he excused himself for a moment and went outside to take the call.

When he returned a few minutes later, his demeanor had completely changed from friendly and welcoming to distant and contrite.

"I'm sorry, Joe," he said, suddenly shifty-eyed, "but it's not going to work out." He raised his eyes just long enough to take in my look of surprise, then lowered them again. He said the call had been from Mr. Green, who told him not only was I untrustworthy, but I had tested positive for HIV.

For a moment I thought he must have been talking about someone else. The subject of HIV had never come up in any context while I was working at the Green Agency—not when I was hired, when I quit to deal with my depression, or when I returned. I felt my face contorting, like it didn't know whether it wanted to smile or snarl. *This guy has got to be kidding.*

One look at Rosenthal's face told me he was very serious. My supervisor had said those things about me, and I was now out of a job.

"What the fuck are you talking about?" I exploded. I might have been slightly manic, but I was also rationally and righteously pissed off.

Rosenthal, on the other hand, looked like he was about to hide under his desk. For the next several minutes, I stood over him, demanding that he tell me every last word Green had said. According to Rosenthal there wasn't much more to tell, and would I please just leave his office now? He was scared to death and no wonder—I was much bigger than he was and barely holding it together.

When I realized he wasn't going to say anything else, I returned to the Green Agency to confront my supervisor. Luckily for him he was out on a sales call, but I found Green in his office. He wasn't surprised to see me, either, because as soon as I left Rosenthal's office, he had called to warn Green that I was looking for him.

He agreed to speak to me, but not before picking up the phone, first to alert security and second to tell his secretary to call 911 if things got out of hand. I almost wanted to laugh—there I was, out of a job because of their lies, but *I* was the threat.

When I calmly asked Green to explain himself, he said he had only repeated to Rosenthal what my supervisor had said to him. Since he was still out of the office, there wasn't much point in my sticking around. As I stood to leave, Green told me to hang on a second, and then I got my next big surprise of the day. He pulled out a piece of paper and wrote down a list of other Equitable agencies I could apply to!

The gesture did little to make me feel better; in fact I left the office devastated. It was the first time I had been discriminated against because of my disease. In the past I had been loved or feared during my manic periods and conspicuously absent from life during my depressions. But no one had ever come out and told me I was unfit to work for them. Even Molly from the nursing home, who'd had every reason to bring up my mental fitness, only pointed to my tardiness when firing me.

I still had no idea how this had come about, but since the story had come from my supervisor, I figured he had started the rumor to cover himself for giving away my leads to his brother. The worst of it was he had assumed he could say anything about me and get away with it because I was bipolar.

With Kevin's help I commenced suit against Equitable, charging them with a violation of the New York State Human Rights Law. My complaint alleged that their actions had caused me additional mental anguish and humiliation as well as monetary loss and damage to my reputation. We also mentioned the list of other agencies Green had suggested I apply to. If I was such a liability, why had he gone out of his way to help me stay with the company?

Equitable's defense was that I had started the HIV rumor myself in order to deflect attention from the bipolar. Had they asserted that claim today, it might have made sense; people with bipolar are viewed as crazy, unstable and—as we've seen in several high profile cases—capable of unspeakable acts of violence. People with HIV, however, are now offered some measure of protection thanks to society's shifting attitudes about that disease. These days no employer in their right mind would tell a person they weren't being hired because they had tested positive.

When this happened back in 1993, however, the situation was completely different. There was still an extreme bias against people who were even suspected of having HIV; they were treated as lepers and often had problems getting or keeping jobs. This was evidenced by the Schulman Agency's refusal to hire me based on my supervisor's unsubstantiated claims. To say I had started such a damaging rumor was nothing short

of ludicrous, but, like my supervisor, Equitable was banking
on the fact that the court would believe them over someone
who admittedly had a mental illness. To bolster this claim,
Green stated in his deposition that he had given me the list of
other agencies only because he was scared for his life. He was
placating me so I would leave his office, then presumably he
would have warned them just as he had the Schulman Agency.

In the end I settled with Equitable for $20,000 despite the
fact that Kevin believed we would have won at trial. Equitable
was clearly in the wrong, but my probationary status made
proving finite economic damages at trial difficult. Twenty
grand was still better than nothing to someone receiving five
hundred a month in SSD benefits. Also, the fact that they paid
at all was somewhat of a vindication not just for me but for
everyone who is discriminated against for having a mental
condition. With this in mind, I tried to move on without being
sucked into another full-blown depression.

I was still cycling when Stephen graduated from college in
December 1992. By that time he too had had a falling out with
Dad, who would not even allow him into the house to collect
his personal belongings. "You guys are my enemies," Dad had
announced, once again taking no responsibility for anything
that had gone on between us. Even Stephen, who had left my
mother's house to go live with him, was to blame.

Stephen showed up in Merrick with the clothes on his back
and not much else. This was fine with Kevin and me, who were
already sharing Kevin's crowded bedroom. That first night,
when Mom came to "tuck us in," she didn't even try to hide her

smile. It had come full circle—my father had ripped us apart all those years ago, and now, through his abandonment of yet another son, he had brought us back together again.

I was just drifting off to sleep when I felt Steve, who was lying next to me, roll over. "Don't hog the bed," he warned, "and don't snore."

I grunted in reply and closed my eyes again.

But Stephen wasn't finished. "Oh, and by the way, I never got to thank you for convincing me to come live with you and those two fucking lunatics on Staten Island."

With that the room erupted into laugher. For years we had pretended that life at Dad's house was normal, and it felt so good to let it all hang out finally. In that moment it just all seemed so comical. I didn't know about my brothers, but I hadn't laughed that hard in years, even when I was at my most manic.

We were so loud my mother and Beave could hear us from their bedroom down the hall. "Go to sleep, boys," she yelled, "and no whispering, or I'm getting the Hot Wheels whip."

That only set us off more. We were kids again, getting in trouble after playing Mean Joe Green and trying to pry up the boards in the Vecchios' house. The room was overflowing with our stuff, and my snoring was louder than a busted chainsaw, but that night we got the best sleep since Canarsie.

The joy of our reunion turned out to be short-lived. Just a few days after Steve moved in with us, Grandpa Jack finally succumbed to his decades-long battle with Parkinson's disease. He was eighty-nine and had lived far longer than anyone expected, considering he had suffered with tremors since the 1950s, but that did little to ease our broken hearts. Whereas my mother and Kevin grieved the loss of his constant presence in their lives, I felt bitter about all the years I had missed.

It also brought up all the old feelings of guilt that I had not made more of an attempt to see my Paladino grandparents over the years. The fact that my father had orchestrated the separation didn't make me feel any better about it. Our only solace came from knowing that Grandpa Jack had lived to see us all back together again. For years he and Grandma Dar had longed for our reunion, and now we couldn't help but think that Grandpa Jack had held on just long enough to see this dream become a reality.

At his wake we placed near his coffin a black-and-white picture of him from the 1940s. He looked like a movie star, and I was overwhelmed with pride and incredibly moved when relative after relative looked at the picture and said, "You are the spitting image of your grandfather."

I also realized I was something of a curiosity. Nearly everyone there was sure to ask how I was feeling, which made me very uncomfortable. I understood their curiosity—I had disappeared from the family a happy albeit quiet child and returned fifteen years later with a mental illness. They were concerned and perhaps trying to understand bipolar better, but it didn't make the questions—or their pitying looks—any easier.

I was grateful that at least my grandfather hadn't understood the severity of my illness; he knew only that I had suffered from a "nervous condition." He was already in his late eighties and suffering from mild dementia when I turned up at their house manic and incessantly spouting gibberish about one thing or another. For reasons I still don't completely understand, Kevin had thought it would make Grandpa Jack feel better to hear that I had had a physical relationship with Rita; maybe he thought it would give my grandfather a sense of justice that his ex-son-in-law had been cuckolded by his own son. Fortunately my mother forbade Kevin from telling Grandpa Jack about it, saying it was not an appropriate topic of discussion. I had to admit it would have been fascinating to listen to Kevin explain the situation to a hard-of-hearing eighty-eight-year-old who spoke broken English, but in the end I agreed with my mother.

Unfortunately for Grandma Dar, the gag order had not applied to her; in fact Mom had been the one who told her the story, or at least she started to. As soon as my grandmother had realized what she was getting at, she threw up her hands and said she didn't want to hear anymore—she was sick enough. One day she would confront my father and stepmother, but for the time being she had to focus all of her energies on my ailing grandfather. True to her word, she nursed him around the clock, and my grandfather went to his grave ignorant of how truly sick my life with my father and Rita had been. My grandmother spent several years in mourning after he passed, and as for me, I still carry around a small photocopy of that picture from the wake. As Mom likes to say, "Joe, you are all Paladino, except of course when you are manic."

That statement, said half in jest, brings up a question

often asked by those closest to me: just who is the real Joe? Is it the depressive personality who says little and often lacks the motivation to wash a dish or mow the lawn? Or is it the mania-fueled, charismatic schmoozer who thinks nothing of buying $60,000 automobiles or demanding professional sports tryouts?

No one has the answer to these questions, least of all me. Many people with bipolar cite a devastating loss of self as one of the worst aspects of the disease. Things that brought them joy—family, friends, and hobbies—no longer matter; some don't even recognize themselves when they look in the mirror. It doesn't matter what they've accomplished in their lives because it all seems insignificant compared to their new label: mentally ill. Some eventually regain a sense of identity but often only after months or even years of meds, ECT, and psychotherapy. However, most will say they are never really who they were before that first depression or manic episode.

As painful as I am sure that is, I cannot relate, nor can I hope to one day uncover who I was before I got sick. Unlike those people, I never even had a chance to develop a self. I was completely under my father's thumb for more than a decade, during which my entire existence was wrapped up in pleasing him. Everything I had done during those years—going to live with him, lying about my mother during the custody battle, and giving up my maternal grandparents—had been for that purpose. I was his firstborn son, the apple of his eye, and, I believed, his future partner in medicine. My father loved sports, so I strove to be the best baseball player in school. It's no accident that when manic, my illusions run to being a professional athlete; in my mind this is still a way I can be seen as worthy of his approval.

This false sense of self was shattered when I witnessed my father's lackluster reaction to my college grades. If I wasn't going to be a doctor, what would I be? I wasn't allowed to date for most of my high school years, so I had very limited experience with girls my own age. I had nothing and was nothing; that first depression—and all the ones that followed—just mirrored that feeling. In fact when I'm depressed, I often feel nothing at all. It is not always an overwhelming sadness; sometimes it's the absence of *all* emotion. No wonder I loved it when I became manic—I believed I could play for the Mets and was able to charm the pants off any girl in the bar. In those moments I was my father's son again.

In 1994, after years of riding the bipolar roller coaster, Normal Joe—the guy I had seen only glimpses of since college, suddenly reappeared. I was no longer the "white male with poor appetite, hyposomnia, suicidal ideation, and constricted affect (lack of demonstrated emotion)" described on numerous hospital intake forms, nor was I the aggressive asshole who purchased cars I couldn't afford and verbally abused anyone in my path. I was simply Joseph DeBlasi.

There was no scientific explanation for my remission—I wasn't on any new meds or undergoing some revolutionary form of ECT or psychotherapy. For some reason my brain chemistry simply righted itself. This is quite common in people with bipolar, but to my family and me it still felt like a holy miracle.

My mood held even after another nasty run-in with dad. When he had cut Stephen, Kevin, and me out of his life, he had also effectively severed our ties with our half- brothers, Matthew and Frank, who were fourteen and sixteen respectively. Since dad wasn't speaking to his parents either, we couldn't count on Grandma Jennie to be the go-between this time. Deciding he had played divide and conquer one too many times, Stephen and I petitioned the family court in Monmouth County, New Jersey, for visitation rights with Frank and Matthew. Kevin, who had just completed his first year of law school, acted as both our attorney and our star witness. He was clearly emotional as he testified to the harm he had suffered as a result of being separated from me and Stephen for all those years.

Our father, who was once again represented by his friend LeMole, stared icily ahead. There wasn't much he could do to refute Kevin's testimony, so instead one of LeMole's associates argued that my mental illness made visitation with my minor half siblings too risky. To illustrate this point, he cited the time I had driven erratically with Matthew and Frank shortly after returning from Acapulco. The judge agreed despite the fact that at the time of the incident, I had not yet had any treatment or even been diagnosed. As soon as he announced the decision denying our petition, Dad stood, smug smile in place, and began walking toward the exit. Just as he pulled the door open, he turned, shot us a scathing look, and muttered, "Assholes" before exiting the courtroom.

In the meantime I was trying to rebuild my life. I was under no illusions that I was cured because there is no cure for bipolar, but I was determined to make the most of normalcy for as long as I had it. Before long I had graduated from Mercy's outpatient day program and began VESCED (state-run vocational training). From there I got temp work and, eventually, a permanent job with Dreyfus, a financial services company. Just a few months earlier, my life had centered around group therapy sessions, meds, and shock treatment. Now I was working on mutual funds and retirement investments. I started in an entry-level position in their Uniondale, Long Island, office, but then I received a promotion and was transferred to the Manhattan branch. I was motivated and enjoyed my work, often rising at 4:30 a.m. so I could get in early. I met and started dating a beautiful model named Jacqueline. Everyone—my mother, my brothers, and my doctors—were thrilled. It looked like I might have a career and a life after all.

This inexplicable period of stability would continue for three years despite the fact that for most of that time I was not compliant with my meds. I even drank alcohol, although my intake was moderate, nothing like my mania-fueled binges in college or those crazy summers at Bar A. Life was beginning to feel wonderfully normal for the first time in years. But we were all being lulled into a false sense of security. Manic depression is an insidious and sneaky disease, known for ripping the rug out from under you when you least expect it.

But I wasn't thinking about that at the time because, in addition to working at Dreyfus, I had enrolled part-time in Hofstra's MBA program. I knew if I wanted to keep moving up the ladder in finance, I would need a master's degree and, eventually, my Series 7 license. When I was hired as a systems analyst at AIG in 1997, I really felt like I was on my way. I began my tenure there truly excited, and—from what I remembered of life before mental illness—something akin to happy.

However, just three weeks into my new position, I found myself once again sinking into a deep depression. I couldn't concentrate at work, and even the simplest activity seemed insurmountable. Normal Joe was gone, and he wouldn't make another appearance for several years.

More than 75 percent of people with bipolar experience relapse, usually after a triggering event similar to the one precipitating any depression or manic period. It can be stressful, like losing a job or a loved one, or positive, such as having a child or getting more responsibility at work. The tricky thing is that you never know when it's coming. For example, why was I able to live normally for three years, getting promotions, going to school, and beginning a relationship, only to have it all fall apart? It was as if I was allowed to reach only so far before getting my hand slapped. The why remains a mystery; however, the research shows that people who, like me, have been resistant to treatment in the past are more likely to relapse, as are people who—again, like me—have had frequent relapses in the past.

Doctors believe that all manic depressives should remain on some sort of maintenance plan throughout periods of stability. The problem is when you're feeling good, the last thing you want to do is stay on the meds, get ECT treatments, or even talk to a shrink. The meds cause acne, diarrhea, and weight gain; the ECT makes you forget things; and the shrink encourages you to relive things you'd rather forget. There was no way I was doing that. But once the depression hit, I no longer had a choice. I left my job, contemplated suicide, and resumed treatment, submitting once more to the careful monitoring of my mood by my doctors and family.

CHAPTER 17

Crazy Eights

I have never been much for numerology, but there is no disputing the almost mystical role the number eight has played in my life. I was born in 1968, kidnapped in 1978, and had my first breakdown in 1988. However, the tumult of 1998 would show my family and me just how ugly bipolar can get. Most of my illness has been spent in varying degrees of depression, but I would spend the bulk of '98 in the grips of an uncontrollable mania that threatened not only my life but the lives of everyone around me.

The year began benignly enough. I'd spent the past few months in and out of Mercy Hospital, and finally the ECT had jolted me out of my depression. When I felt stable enough, Kevin and I decided to go down to Florida for a few days. The sun would do us both some good, and we had been promising to visit our stepsister Beth, who had moved to Melbourne after her divorce.

Our first few days in the Sunshine State were unremarkable. Kevin and I took in the sun and played the doting uncles to Beth's four-year-old daughter, Alesia. But after four days, I had grown bored of Melbourne despite its pristine beaches and Bare Assets, one of the swankier gentlemen's clubs in Brevard County. I was becoming antsy, a sure sign that Manic Joe was about to make an appearance.

Doctors have long recognized the connection between light and mood. Like people with seasonal affective disorder, those with bipolar must be cognizant of the changing seasons as a threat to stability. Too little light can bring on depression just as too much light can bring on mania. The statistics bears this out: most people are hospitalized for mania in the summer while the number of people committed for depression peaks in the late fall. I didn't know whether it was the Florida sun or one too many ECT treatments, but my mood was definitely on an uptick, and it felt wonderful.

Kevin didn't argue when I told him I wanted to head to Miami despite the fact that he knew the trip would drain him, not to mention his wallet. He wisely knew it was easier to join me than to try to chase me around South Florida. For the next few days, we partied hard at South Beach's Clevelander Hotel, and surprisingly returned home with nothing more than the usual vacation stories of twenty-something guys.

Once we returned to New York, however, things began to get out of hand. I dragged Kevin into Manhattan to have dinner with friends I had met while working at Dreyfus. From there we went to Le Bar Bat, a popular nightclub in Midtown. Normally it would have been packed, but since it was midweek and the dead of winter, there weren't many people there. This made it that much easier for us to spot Miami Dolphins quarterback Dan Marino, Ravens defensive linesman Tony Siragusa, and several less known but equally large NFL players. As it turned out, they were in town for a fundraiser—cystic fibrosis or autism, I wasn't sure. After the event they had gone looking for a place to party, which, unfortunately, Le Bar Bat was *not.*

When Kevin asked the bartender where we could go for a better crowd, he didn't hesitate: "Cheetah Club, Forty-Third Street between Seventh and Eighth."

Armed with this insider information, Kevin walked over to Dan Marino, introduced himself, and told him about the Cheetah. Marino graciously thanked him for the tip and said he was waiting for a few more guys but would likely see us there.

By that time my eyes were bothering me, probably because when I'm manic I cannot be bothered with such trivial matters as cleaning my contact lenses. The smoky club didn't help, especially the fat stogie clamped between Siragusa's steely jaws. When I asked him none too politely to put it out, he shot me an annoyed look but walked away without saying anything. I then joined Kevin, who was still talking to Dan Marino. My brother, known for his ability to talk the ass off a camel, had Marino in stitches. After telling him that Grandpa Frank watched only

NFL games featuring an Italian quarterback, Kevin inquired as to whether Marino had any interest in playing for New York. When Marino responded he would love to play for Jets coach Bill Parcells, Kevin didn't miss a beat: "That fat fuck Parcells has bigger breasts than any broad in this place. You should play for the Giants." Marino was still laughing as we all headed out the door and grabbed a couple of cabs to the Cheetah.

Both Kevin and I are fairly big guys, so the bouncers at the Cheetah assumed we were part of the NFL contingent. Kevin, who was thrilled that we didn't have to stand on line or pay the twenty-five-dollar cover, couldn't stop talking about how cool Dan Marino was. Had Normal Joe been there, he would have felt the same; Manic Joe, on the other hand, couldn't have cared less about meeting a legendary quarterback. He was much more concerned with the scantily clad women prancing around the club. With my South Beach tan, Grandpa Jack's blue eyes, and a confident swagger, I was soon talking up two beauties like *I* was the celebrity.

Everything was great until one of the bouncers came over and told me Kevin and I had to leave. "You are stalking the NFL players, and that guy over there wants you gone." I followed the bouncer's thick finger to find Siragusa holding the cigar in one hand and waving good-bye to us with the other. It was obviously payback for mouthing off to him about the stogie at Le Bar Bat.

The rage, always simmering just below the surface during a manic period, came on hard and fast. No matter that Siragusa was more than three hundred pounds or that the bouncer had arms like a giant sequoia; I was ready to take on them and anyone else who stood between the DeBlasi brothers and a night of partying. Just before things got ugly, Dan Marino stepped in. He explained that we were not stalkers but the reason he and the other players had come to Cheetah in the first place. He then apologized for Siragusa, saying he was not always such a jerk.

Eternally grateful to Marino for preventing my arrest and a likely hospitalization as well, Kevin used the twenty-five bucks he had saved at the door to buy him an overpriced drink at the bar. He may never have won a Super Bowl, but from that moment on Dan Marino was a hero in our family, and Grandpa Frank never missed another Dolphins game.

A year later Siragusa and some other players would return to New York for the same fundraiser. Later that night they made the news for an altercation at Hogs & Heifers, a landmark bar in the Meatpacking District. Several witnesses, including former Jet Wayne Chrebet, commented that Siragusa had been out of line. Although I was depressed at the time, I managed a rare smile at the thought of Kevin and me dancing between the NFL stars a year earlier. I can't say for sure when I began to obsess about playing for the Jets, but I would guess that being mistaken for an NFL player that cold January night had something to do with it.

By March 3rd I found myself back at Mercy Hospital. I had been manic for months but not completely out of control. By February, however, my mood had been steadily elevating; I had been becoming more irritable, and any money I had was burning a hole in my pocket, much of it on cell phone bills. I had recently developed a habit of calling everyone I had ever known, often keeping them on the phone for hours with a never-ending stream of consciousness.

All hell really broke loose, however, when Jacqueline and I had taken a short trip to Puerto Rico. On our first night there, I had spent every dime I had on gambling and expensive meals. Over the course of the next three days, I would spend an additional $400 on telephone calls. I was extremely agitated the entire time and threatened Jacqueline when she refused to give me her credit card. By the time we returned to New York, she was terrified.

As soon as Kevin and Mom saw the state I was in, they took me straight to Mercy, where the staff noted my "menacing and threatening" behavior and delusions of grandeur. Dr. Teitelbaum recommended that I be admitted, but I refused, stating there was nothing wrong with me—this despite the fact that I had recently contracted to buy another $60,000 car and was claiming to have earned millions of dollars on the stock market. The only way I would consent to hospitalization was if another doctor concurred with Dr. Teitelbaum's assessment. To this day I'm not sure why they allowed me to walk out of there, but they did after arranging an appointment for my second opinion.

The next day Mom and I returned to meet with Dr. Kothari. Knowing that my freedom depended on his assessment, I adopted a much more pleasant demeanor than I'd had with Teitelbaum. I even admitted to being slightly up but said I had been taking my meds—a lie that my mother quickly refuted. Then, in an effort to convince Dr. Kothari how together I was, I picked up the phone to call my broker. I wanted to discuss how wealthy I was and prove I could buy and sell any stock I wanted. I was still congratulating myself on a stellar performance when, to my surprise, Dr. Kothari diagnosed me as manic with psychosis—a new one for me. When I still wouldn't consent to hospitalization, he strongly suggested to Mom that I be admitted under section 939 of the Mental Hygiene Law, meaning I posed a substantial risk to myself and others.

Once admitted I spit out the first round of meds and continued to refuse them for the entire first day. I also told my Mom and Kevin that I was going to hurt the doctor, and, what's more, I wouldn't be working with Teitelbaum any longer. In fact I was going to use my considerable wealth to ruin him. "I'm a lawyer," I announced to another staff member, "and I'm going to sue all of you."

By that afternoon I had calmed down but became out of control again when Jacqueline visited. She looked on wide-eyed as I screamed that nothing was wrong with me and demanded to be released or else. She had witnessed my mood swings before, but this was the first time she had seen me this manic—and this scary.

"I love Joe," she confessed to one of the nurses, "but I don't know if I could handle a future with him." Why she was saying this, I couldn't imagine. I had no desire to hurt anyone; I just didn't want to be held against my will. For the next several days, I tortured the staff, threatening violence and lawsuits, telling them, "I can buy and sell you" and picking and choosing what meds I would take.

Eventually I was stable enough to be released, but the nightmare was just beginning. My obsession had shifted from money to a singular fixation on becoming a pro athlete, specifically with the New York Jets. It was all I could think about, and—unfortunately for Kevin—it was all I could talk about as well. Dan Marino might have said he'd like to play for Bill Parcells, but in 1998 I probably would have *killed* to play for him.

After I'd staked out their camp for months, Jets officials finally gave me paperwork to fill out for my tryout. Unable to sit still, I told Kevin and Mom that I was going to bring the paperwork back to them that night. I had convinced myself that in addition to going out for fullback, my arm was good enough to play quarterback as well. I dragged Kevin outside, intent on showing him my arm strength and accuracy. After three tries, I was able to throw the football and hit the stop sign at the end of the street from about forty yards. Surely, I thought, this was enough to demonstrate my professional quarterbacking ability. Kevin then picked up the football and, on his first try, threw a perfect spiral, hitting the bull's-eye stop sign. He turned to me with a raised eyebrow, thinking it would show me how ridiculous I was being. But instead of seeing his throw as a lucky break, I exclaimed, "You can be my backup!"

Shaking his head, Kevin went back in the house, refusing to accompany me to the training facility. Mom, afraid of what would happen if I went alone, said she would go.

It was after 10:00 p.m. when we got to the training camp,

just in time to see Bill Parcells walking alone across the dimly lit lot. I immediately threw the car in park and jumped out, leaving Mom behind. "Bill," I shouted to Parcells, who looked rather alarmed by seeing a tall, muscular guy racing toward him. "I got the papers for you. I'm ready for Sunday, and we are going to kill 'em!"

Parcells took the papers from me, looked quizzically at the embossed Jets letterhead, and said, "I don't know who you are or if you are here to kill me."

Now it was my turn to be surprised. "I'm not here to hurt you, Bill. I'm here to help you win Sunday. I'll kill for you."

By that time Mom had gotten out of the car and was running over, shouting, "He's my son, Joseph DeBlasi, and he won't hurt anyone!"

Parcells said nothing, just stared at Mom as though she were as crazy as I. Then a look of relief crossed his face when he saw Jets official JoJo Wooden appear.

"That's Steve's guy," Wooden shouted from across the lot. He was referring to Jets security head Steve Yarnell, who, thanks to Kevin, was coordinating my tryout.

No longer afraid, Parcells threw the paperwork I had given him in Wooden's direction. "JoJo," he said, "take care of this. I don't have time for this shit." He then stalked off without so much as a good-bye to Mom and me.

The rest of 1998 was a blur of grandeur and rage for me; for everyone else it was a time of unprecedented fear and stress. In April I was once again admitted to Mercy, where I was nearly choked to death by a staff member. The resulting lawsuit made things awkward for my mother, who still worked there, and impacted her decision to retire early.

In September I hired a limo to take me all the way to Cape Cod, where my brother Stephen was getting married. I could not afford the $1,100 it cost; however, it was better than the $4,000 I had originally been quoted, as I had wanted them to drive me around all weekend. I arrived at the Cape aggressive and obnoxious then spent the next two days cycling so many times I lost count. From hour to hour, I didn't know whether I would be manic and out of control or morbidly depressed. I came very close to ruining the whole affair, especially when I decided to join the a cappella singing group Stephen and his bride had as entertainment.

As if my family didn't have enough to deal with, I also had a partner in crime. My old friend Mike Miccio was also in the full throes of mania for most of that year, and he was at my side for most of my exploits. We were like two wild, overgrown adolescents, dividing our time between his house in Staten Island and my mother's house on Long Island. We were also regular troublemakers in Atlantic City, and it wasn't long before the staff of the Taj Mahal banned us from the premises. Had Mom and Beave not been afraid for us and *of* us, they likely would have done the same at their house.

The year of hell culminated at Christmas Eve dinner, when I flew into a rage and choked Beave. He and Mom called the police, and I spent the rest of the holiday enduring the deplorable conditions at Hempstead General. I wouldn't have wished a stay there on anyone except perhaps the staff, who treated us like we were animals in a zoo. By the end of December, my mother and stepfather were forced to take out an order of protection against me; even Beave had reached the end of his rope. They decided to sell the house in Merrick and move down to Melbourne, where they would be close to Beave's daughter and granddaughter. So much for a fresh start, though, because I followed them down to Florida. Before I left New York in 1999, I broke up with Jacqueline, who had stuck by me through my many meltdowns over the previous year.

For the next year and a half, I travelled between Florida and New York as if a change in scenery would somehow help me escape myself. After nearly twelve straight months of mania, my moods had begun their endless cycling again, and as Mom and Beave tried to adjust to their new life in Melbourne, they never knew which Joe was going to show up on their doorstep: monosyllabic, sad Joe; charming and ambitious Joe; or, worst of all, aggressive and threatening Joe. Moreover, the person they said good night to was oftentimes not the same person who came out for breakfast. The fact that I didn't have regular doctors in Florida and was often noncompliant with my meds didn't help matters any. Dr. Teitelbaum was always kept in the loop, however, and when I look at my treatment records from that time, I'm amazed he didn't lose *his* mind trying to keep track of my condition.

As before, my depressions were treated with ECT; when manic I often refused treatment, and my delusions remained squarely focused on becoming a pro athlete. My experience with the Jets had done nothing to squash that; it had merely shifted my obsession, albeit temporarily, from football to baseball. This would eventually lead to my infamous run-in with the Mets and the Port St. Lucie police in February 2000, followed a few days later by the attack on Mom and my subsequent arrest.

After convincing the staff at Circles of Care psychiatric facility of my sanity, I was facing the very scary reality of prison. When I was returned to Sharpes, the guards, aware of my bipolar, placed me in protective custody. I didn't mind this so much until it was time for lights out, and I was handed a paper gown: standard sleep attire for those with mental issues. The rationale was that if I had no place to hide any weapons, there was less chance of me committing suicide in the middle of the night. I wasn't even allowed to have shoelaces!

Trying to sleep that night was a fruitless endeavor. Not only was I in jail, I was severely manic and suffering from sleep apnea as well. I tossed and turned for hours before finally passing out from sheer exhaustion. I must have continued thrashing about in my sleep, though, because when I awoke the next morning I was completely naked, and there were shreds of paper gown flung all over the cell.

The irony of prison is that while the guards were bound and determined to protect me from myself, they were not so concerned with protecting me from the other prisoners, most of them hardened by their lives of crime. As soon as the guards determined I was not a threat to myself or others, I was moved to general population and into a cell inhabited by a guy known as the Freezer Man. He had gotten the name because allegedly that was where the police had found his last victim. No one knew for sure, and I wasn't about to question him.

Freezer Man did have a question for me, however: "You snore?"

When I admitted that I did, he kindly recommended that I transfer cells so he wouldn't have to kill me during the night. Grateful for the warning, I did just that. I might have been manic, but I wasn't stupid.

Instead I was at my charismatic best. Later that day I was shooting hoops out in the yard with some of the other guys. After snagging several rebounds and scoring a few put backs—all while barefoot, as protective custody had yet to return my sneakers and their potentially lethal laces—my fellow inmates accepted me. In fact a less athletic guy was ordered to take off his sneakers and hand them over to me. As my family always says, it was by the grace of God that I wasn't depressed at Sharpes. Manic and muscular, I was not only able to survive, but made allies that kept me safe until my brother Stephen flew down to Florida and bailed me out.

The criminal charges were diverted, and I was ordered into anger management. However, it did not manage the anger as much as redirect it. As soon as I returned to New York, I showed up at my father's Staten Island medical practice and demanded to see him. Miccio had recently been given a new medication for mania with great success. I wanted my father to get me admitted to Staten Island Hospital for the same treatment.

His response: get lost. When Grandma Jennie called

him on my behalf, he hung up on her. I was enraged. When depressed I blame myself for the events of my childhood—for deserting my mother during the custody battle, for carrying on with Rita, and most of all for not being the son Dad wanted. But whenever Manic Joe returns, he reminds me where the fault really lies, and I often feel compelled to remind my father as well.

CHAPTER 18

The Immaculate Load

Unlike Grandpa Jack, Grandma Dar was keenly aware of the severity of my illness and worried constantly for my well-being and that of my primary caretakers, Mom and Kevin. Knowing that money—or the lack thereof—was a constant source of stress, she was always there to provide a financial hand. A Saint Joseph's day didn't pass without her sending me a "little something"—a tradition that continues to this day. Many times that little something is the only thing in my wallet.

Grandma never questioned me about what had happened when I lived with Dad and Rita, and I certainly never brought it up. So I was surprised when she called me at Kevin's apartment and said, "I have some business to discuss with your father. Will you boys drive me to his office?" Shocked, I said we would, then she added, "You boys will wait in the car for me. I don't want you fighting with him." They say everyone has their limit, and apparently Grandma Dar had hit hers when she'd learned that I had wrapped her daughter in a mattress and threatened to throw her over the balcony, and spent a month in a Florida jail on an assault charge.

Kevin and I agreed to her terms, but we were concerned about her. Sure, underneath her demure demeanor Grandma Dar was as tough as Grandma Jennie; however, Grandma Dar was older—eighty-six at that time—and had recently had a stent placed in her heart. She also had years of pent-up anger at my father for hurting her daughter and grandsons. There was no way Kevin and I were going to let her confront him alone.

Miccio, who lived a few miles from Dad's office, was our first choice to go in with her. But he refused, saying he did not want to anger a doctor on staff at Staten Island Hospital; he worried that our father would use his influence with the psychiatrists to lock him up and give him "a freakin' lobotomy."

Miccio then suggested a friend of his known only as the Duke. Another hard-knocks Brooklyn guy in his mid-fifties, the Duke was like Miccio minus the mania. He might have stood only five foot four and weighed 140 pounds, but he was larger than life. He also wore enough gold jewelry to make Mr. T jealous and had a metal plate in his head from a motorcycle accident. People who knew the Duke said two things about him: he could give an aspirin a headache, and he would do anything for a friend. One call from Miccio and he was more than willing to accompany Grandma Dar to our father's office; intimidating the great Dr. DeBlasi would be the icing on the cake.

As promised Kevin and I drove them, staring in amazement as the rough-hewn Duke escorted my dignified grandmother to the building and held the door open for her. Once inside Grandma Dar went right up to the front desk. "I'm here to see the doctor. Tell him it's Mrs. Jack Paladino." When the receptionist, assuming she was just another one of Dad's elderly patients, started to explain away the long wait, Duke stepped in.

"She's not a patient. She's his ex-mother-in-law."

"And who are *you*?" the woman asked, raising an eyebrow at him.

"I'm the Duke," he replied as if that was all she needed to know. "Now go get the doctor. Mrs. Paladino is waiting."

Quickly realizing she wanted no further involvement with this situation, the woman hurried to one of the examining rooms to tell Dad. A moment later she was back, looking a little nervous.

"I'm sorry, but the doctor won't be able to see you. As you can see, he has all these patients waiting here for him."

Sensing Duke was about to erupt, Grandma shot him a look. She would handle this. Then she calmly made her way to the throng of patients sitting in the waiting room, announced herself as Dr. DeBlasi's former mother-in-law, and began telling them all about the good doctor—how he had cheated on her daughter then left her with three infant sons only to kidnap the oldest later and brainwash him against her. The patients, most of who had probably been going to my father for years, just stared at her in confusion. Grandma Dar was just about to tell them what had gone on between Rita and me when Dad emerged. My grandmother hadn't seen him in nearly thirty years and was taken aback by his appearance.

"He is immense," she later told us. "And in that white coat, he looks as big as an iceberg."

Not wanting any more of his dirty laundry aired, Dad quickly ushered my grandmother and the Duke into his office. Grandma Dar looked around pointedly at the diplomas and licenses her daughter had helped him secure, then took a seat across the desk from him,

My father eyed Duke as he would have a common criminal. "Who are you?"

"Don't worry about who I am," Duke said calmly. "Just listen to what Grandma has to say."

Dad turned back to Grandma Dar. "What do you want?"

"Joe needs your help. He is sick. You are a doctor and his father. You and your wife made him sick, and now you have to help. Regina has been doing everything she can, but she can't anymore. If you *don't* help, we are going to expose you and your wife."

My father shook his head. "I won't help him after what he did to my wife."

"What *he* did to *her*?"

My father's face twisted with disgust. "He would look at her and get so excited that he blew a load in his pants! Joey would just look at her and blow a load."

The room fell into an icy silence. Even the Duke was stunned, not only by my father's ridiculous explanation of the events but by the coarse language he had used in front of his former mother-in-law.

My grandmother took a few moments to compose herself, then said, "Nonsense, Joseph. Your wife had more than a hand in it. She is a pedophile."

When he heard that word, my father turned bright red, like he always did when he was extremely angry. I don't know whether it was out of respect for my grandmother or out of fear of the Duke, but he did not scream as he usually did when Rita was accused of molesting me. Instead he just leaned across the desk and gently took Grandma Dar's hand.

"Clara, you know me. I'm Sicilian. If I thought for one second that my wife did anything wrong...." He pulled his hand back and dragged it across his throat. "I'd slit her from ear to ear."

Realizing she was dealing with someone even sicker than I was, Grandma Dar calmly motioned to Duke that it was time to go. Just as she reached the door, she turned to my father and said, "Joseph, sharpen your knife."

When she and the Duke emerged from the building, Kevin and I were relieved to see that she seemed no worse for the wear. At first she said nothing about what had gone on inside, just requested that we drop the Duke off at his apartment. He was clearly in awe of her, repeating, "Joe, you got a stand-up Grandma" several times during the ride. He also filled Kevin and me in on the conversation they had had in the office, including what Kevin would come to refer to as my father's "immaculate load theory." We wanted to hear more about it, but that would have to wait. After dropping the Duke off, we were headed down to Holmdel so Grandma could talk with Rita.

For years Kevin had heard that friends of Grandma Dar's had seen Dad and Rita at some social event and were less than impressed by Rita's looks. Maybe these people were just trying to soften the blow, knowing how difficult the divorce had been on my mother and grandparents. Sure enough, as we sped over the Outerbridge Crossing—one of the three bridges linking Staten Island and New Jersey—Grandma Dar recounted that story, adding details that were new even to my brother. It had been a Sicilian-American gathering held in Canarsie in the mid-1970s, not long after our father had married Rita. Grandpa Frank and Grandma Jennie had been in attendance as well as Grandma Dar's friend. When Grandma Dar repeated how her friend had thought Mom was much prettier than Rita and that Rita was very plain, Kevin was unable to resist making a sarcastic remark.

"She couldn't be so plain, Grandma, because Joe would just look at her and get so excited that right in his pants...."

I knew I should have felt embarrassed that my brother was joking about this in front of Grandma Dar, but after everything I had been through, I only felt numb. Besides, it took all my mental energy to concentrate on finding Dad and Rita's house. I hadn't been to Holmdel in years.

Finally we pulled up to a house that I was 95 percent sure was theirs. This time Grandma did not make us stay in the car. The three of us walked up to the front door, then she rang the bell. No answer. She pressed it a few more times. Still no answer.

"I know she is in there," Grandma Dar insisted. "Let's go around back."

We knew that tone well; it was the same tone Grandma Dar had used when we were naughty as kids. It left no room for argument. When we reached the back door, she began pounding on it. "Open up! I want to talk to you. I know you're in there, you *disgratzia!*"

No one came to the door, and to this day we don't know whether Rita was really out or if she was hiding inside, just as she and I had hid from the cops shortly after I was kidnapped. Still, I had to hand it to Grandma Dar. After nearly three decades of waiting, she was determined to say her piece. Thanks to the Duke, she'd had some success with my father, but in New Jersey she would have to settle for pounding on a back door. However, we left there with no doubts in our minds; as Duke had said several times in the car, we indeed had a "stand-up grandma." She wasn't done with them, either. She later returned to Dad's office, this time with my mother, to ask him again to help me get treatment. This time he would not see them and even called the police. Thankfully the cops decided not to arrest Mom and Grandma Dar but ordered them to leave immediately.

My father's refusal to help me get treatment was the final straw not only for my grandmother but for my mother, Kevin, and me. Deciding it was time to crack the façade of respectability that he and Rita had carefully constructed, we returned to his office once again, but this time it wasn't to talk to him—it was to hold a protest rally. Joined by Aunt Paula and a dozen or so friends including the Duke, we held signs exposing the real Joseph and Rita DeBlasi. Miccio continued to admire our efforts from a distance, again citing his fear of doctors and lobotomies. He understood where we were coming from, as he too had had a falling out with his scumbag father, a prominent vintner who had become famous—and quite wealthy—turning bad wine to good.

During the protest we met several people who showed much interest and even compassion for us. Some of them were my father's patients, and they were shocked to learn that the charming doctor they had known for years could treat his sons—particularly one suffering from mental illness—with such malice and neglect. A few people even suggested we report him to the state medical ethics board, pointing out that if he could treat his own flesh and blood this way, he could not be trusted to make rational medical decisions for others. Still others promised to return for a second rally we were planning. This surprised even us given the fact that Staten Island could be likened to a small town, and our father had substantial clout there.

The police were called, but as long as we did not block the entrance we were afforded the same First Amendment rights as anyone protesting a cause. We did have to take our signs off the wooden stakes; however, we then passed out flyers summarizing everything Dad and Rita had done to me. Throughout it all Dad never emerged from his office, relying instead on some of his most loyal patients to defend him and Rita. As a result a few shouting matches broke out between us and them, but with Grandma Dar there cooler heads always prevailed before it could escalate into a physical altercation.

When he realized he couldn't stop us himself, Dad called LeMole. Knowing that Kevin was instrumental in coordinating the rallies, LeMole filed an order of protection against both of us. In the papers Dad alleged that Kevin and I were threatening to kill him despite the fact that neither of us had spoken to him. Since I was always changing residences, Dad and LeMole were unable to serve the order on me; however, they easily found Kevin at his East Meadow law office. He was soon back on Staten Island, but this time it was to go to court.

Grandma Dar went with him, planning to testify that she had been with him during the entire rally and that he had not even seen his father, let alone threatened him. But things hadn't changed much since the custody case in 1978; it was still no use fighting LeMole in a Staten Island court. The judge refused to hear Grandma's testimony and admonished Kevin, even threatening to report him to the New York bar for disciplinary action. With his legal career in jeopardy, Kevin capitulated, and the rallies ceased. We couldn't help but see the irony in the situation: nearly three decades earlier, Dad had hired LeMole to get me to live with him; now he was hiring him to keep his sons one hundred feet away. How I wished he had just left us all alone when we were kids! We would have recovered from the divorce and his defection from the family.

However, his endless manipulation—not to mention his decision to believe Rita's version of our relationship—has been far more detrimental.

In May 2000 I showed up at Teitelbaum's office with what he referred to, in his understated way, as "multiple problems." Not only had I gotten into a fight at a bar, but I'd been caught sneaking into the gym at Hofstra, where I had continued to work out despite being banned from campus in 1998. Campus police let me go but promised to have me arrested if they ever saw my face there again. I had started seeing Jacqueline again, but, as I told Dr Teitelbaum, "I want to be with her, but I don't think it's good for her to be around me. I never know what my mood is going to be."

I was also facing serious financial issues. Back in early 1998, I had exhausted my short-term disability from AIG, the job I was forced to leave when my three-year period of stability ended. At that time my long-term policy with First Unum kicked in; however, like most carriers, First Unum had a mental illness exclusion that limited collection to two years. Under this exclusion they cut off my benefits in early 2000, claiming the bipolar was a mental rather than a physical condition. That meant I was eligible for only $1,100 a month in Social Security—hardly enough to support myself.

But those things were trivial compared to the feelings of rage I still had for Dad. When I told Teitelbaum about the scene at the medical office and the resulting order of protection, he advised me to distance myself from my problems with my father. I could continue to talk about my issues in therapy, but I had to stop trying to see him or get any satisfaction from him. It wasn't going to work, and it would land me back in the hospital or, worse, jail. Sitting in Teitelbaum's office, that made sense, especially since I had to admit that an apology from my father or Rita wouldn't quite cut it. When Manic Joe takes over, however, I really don't care about what makes sense: I want what I want when I want it.

Instead Teitelbaum advised me to up my meds and avoid all stress. I yessed him to death because my real concern was football. I was still hoping to get an agent and play in the NFL. I held it together through June and most of July, when my mood started to drop. By August I had sunken into another severe depression. Unable to care for myself, I had to go to Florida so Mom and Beave could care for me. They made sure I bathed, ate, and didn't try to kill myself. I came out of my bedroom only for meals and doctor appointments and didn't speak unless spoke to.

I would remain depressed to varying degrees for the next several years; however, there were brief periods of relief and some mania, during which I tried unsuccessfully to hold down a job. In February 2001 I started working at a department store, then was hired by Morgan Stanley as a financial analyst. I even began studying to get my Series 7 license. That all went out the window when I heard the Florida Marlins were holding tryouts. I quit Morgan Stanley immediately, thinking I was on my way to a pro baseball career as third baseman. I got to the tryout late, and they hit me some grounders at short. Since these were walk-on tryouts, at least there was no altercation with security as there had been with the Mets.

That summer I tried traditional work again. I had gone

back to New York to attend Kevin's wedding and stayed, taking a job selling prepaid legal insurance policies. It sounded promising but turned out to be a pyramid scheme that required me to buy a license to sell the policies then sell the rights to sell the insurance to five or more others. I didn't sell one policy and lost the money I had invested. From there I tried my hand at telemarketing for a sports betting company. That lasted all of six weeks and took me into my next deep depression.

My doctors suggested I go back for more ECT, but my family disagreed, not wanting to risk the mania. Jacqueline, who I was living with, had also had her fill of Manic Joe. She nixed the ECT but promised to make sure I got out of the house every day. Despite her efforts I spent the next six months sleeping, watching TV, and thinking up creative ways to end it all. A brief respite in March 2002 gave me a few months to ask her to marry me and to work as a personal trainer for eight dollars an hour.

I continued to cycle for all of 2003. For months I was so depressed, I couldn't lift my head from the pillow. I was even suffering a mild depression at my wedding in November 2003, and our house—purchased by Jacqueline with help from Mom and Grandma Dar—had to be put in Jacqueline's name for fear that I would lose it during a manic episode. It was during one of those ups when I had my next encounter with Dad.

Feeling antsy, I headed to his office one day with no real agenda other than to remind him that his past mistakes were not going away no matter how many big houses he built or awards he received. As soon as he saw me enter the waiting room, Dad disappeared into his office. I followed and found him rummaging through the desk. He then pulled out some papers, which he began reading to me: "If Joseph DeBlasi Jr. comes within one hundred feet of Joseph DeBlasi Sr., DeBlasi Jr. will be arrested." It was the order of protection he had filed but never properly served on me back in 2000. I looked him straight in the eye and told him he could shove the papers up his ass and that he and LeMole were idiots for not being able to serve me.

For once my father let the mask drop. "Please, Joey, just go. I don't want to see you getting arrested. The cops are on the way."

After he asked for the third time, I surprised him—and myself—by leaving. Maybe I felt sorry for him, or maybe I just didn't want to relive my month at Sharpes. Mom and Beave firmly believed it was the latter; they had told me more than once that Sharpes had taught even Manic Joe a lesson. I didn't know about that; I was just forever grateful to Stephen for bailing me out before something bad happened.

When I fell into another deep depression in January 2004, my family sent me to see Dr. Fieve, who was known as the godfather of bipolar disorder. His solution was to switch me back to lithium, which I had been on when I'd first gotten sick but hadn't taken for many years. I then went back to Dr. Teitelbaum but continued on Fieve's med regimen.

I don't know if it was the lithium, but in 2005 my mood began to stabilize once more. I hadn't felt that good since 1997.

This time Normal Joe stuck around for two years, even after I stopped taking the meds. There was one significant difference, though: the ambition I'd had in the '90s was long gone, beaten out of me by dozens of cycles. No one expected me to begin a new career or go back to Hofstra; everyone, including me, was content with the fact that I wasn't thinking of killing myself or gambling away the mortgage in Atlantic City.

It seemed like more good news was on the horizon when I received a letter from First Unum. I had been living hand to mouth since 2000, when my First Unum long-term disability had run out. As part of a multistate settlement with the insurance regulators and the United States Department of Labor, First Unum had cut a deal with the government, agreeing to reassess all policyholders whose disability benefits had been declined since 2000. Realizing that I needed specialized legal representation, I gave a $5,000 retainer to Quadrino and Schwartz, a firm known for its thriving disability and Employee Retirement Income Security Act (ERISA) practice.

During the reassessment period, Mike Hack of Quadrino and Schwartz filed a class action lawsuit against First Unum alleging systemic procedural ERISA violations in their claims-review process. Hack used me as the named plaintiff in the class action, which I readily consented to as I wanted to do my part in advocating for the mentally ill. Hack won the action, and Quadrino and Schwartz were granted $50,000 in attorneys' fees. All the plaintiffs were granted access to First Unum's files regarding why their original claims had been denied.

It was a huge victory—or seemed like one until my

reassessment was denied in 2006. While my claim was being reassessed by First Unum, the Second Circuit came out with a decision supporting First Unum's position that bipolar disorder was a mental disease (*Fuller v. J.P. Morgan Chase* 423 F. 3D 104). I not only lost the case and my $5,000 retainer, but I also received a letter from the IRS declaring me responsible for paying the taxes on the $50,000 Quadrino had recovered in attorneys' fees.

Frantic and completely blindsided by the tax bill, I placed several calls to the law firm. After a few weeks of phone tag, I went to the office to speak to Hack in person. Thankfully I wasn't manic, or it might have gotten ugly. Up to that point, Hack and his staff had been extremely competent and diligent; I simply couldn't believe they were allowing me to twist in the wind with their tax bill, especially since they knew all I had gone through. After months of anguish and meetings with accountants, the tax bill was finally straightened out. Still, the stress had taken quite a toll on both Jacqueline and me.

As in most cases, at least those I have experienced, it had all come down to money. Perhaps if I had earned more at AIG and was therefore receiving a bigger disability check, I would have had my private disability reinstated. However, Quadrino and Schwartz did not see a big payout at the end of the day and were willing only to submit papers for the reassessment rather than waging an expensive all-out lawsuit.

This issue is larger than my case. Most mentally ill people do not have the financial resources to hire the crack attorneys needed to obtain justice in the courts. Thanks to my family, I am more fortunate than most; for example I was able to hire the private criminal attorney who got my domestic-relations charges dropped without probation and without it going on my permanent record. This meant it would not show up on background checks when I applied for jobs. Many people with bipolar are first penalized for their illness by being sent to jail then must carry the label of "criminal" around for the rest of their lives.

In 2007 Normal Joe ran for the hills again, and I was back to endless cycles peppered by brief periods of calm. In 2008 Jacqueline and I had a child, which, given my history, was a blessing I never could have anticipated.

I'd had nothing to do with my father in years, but that didn't mean my anger for him wasn't lurking in the back of my mind. After a phone call in 2010 from Miccio, in which he told me Dad had been lauded once more in the newspaper for his doctoring, my thoughts again turned to how I could get under the old man's skin. At that time I was living way out on Long Island, and even though I was manic I didn't relish the idea of a two-hour drive to his office. How did I solve this dilemma? I called in a bomb threat to his office from my cell phone. When Kevin explained to me that post-9/11 any such threats—even those made in jest—meant jail time, I pressed "redial" and repeated the threat to my father's stunned receptionist. When I'm manic I don't care about consequences; I wanted to cause my father some trouble, and not even the electric chair would have deterred me.

For the most part, though, Kevin has learned how to defuse my mania-fueled episodes before they get out of control. "Joe, if you check yourself in right now to Stony Brook Psych Unit," he told me the night of the bomb threat, "I think we can keep you out of jail."

"No fucking way. I'm starving. Hospital food sucks."

"No problem," he replied, not missing a beat. "We'll go pick up a pot of linguini and white clam sauce from Maroni's, and we can eat it in the waiting room while they're doing your admission paperwork."

Maroni's, one of my favorite Italian restaurants on Long Island, is famous for packing its to-go dishes in huge white pots. Somehow Kevin knew that the thought of the two of us hanging out in the hospital waiting room while spooning down clams from a Maroni pot, would appeal to me. We picked up our food and headed to the hospital, where I consented to being admitted for mania—a real feat considering how hard it had been in the past. Kevin's pasta trick got me out of trouble that night, and, even though I was later transferred from the plush Stony Brook facility to the horrors of a psych unit in Amityville, it was still the Waldorf compared to Sharpes.

There are many people who have cared for me throughout my illness, and I owe all of them my life. However, no one, not even my doctors, understands my illness better than Kevin. Ever since Grandma Jennie orchestrated our reunion, we have had a special bond—I think it's because Kevin went through the same painful separation from both of his brothers. Whatever the case, neither of us believes it's a coincidence that Stephen, the most well-adjusted of us, was never forced to live as an only child.

Kevin has never doubted that my traumatic childhood

was and continues to be a significant factor in my illness. His research over the years has borne this out; the events after my parents' divorce not only played a role in triggering the bipolar but are the reason my depressions are so severe and long-lasting. The best analogy would be a football player who suffers the cumulative effects of the many concussions he has had over the course of his career. Similarly, the aggregate of my "concussions"—being coerced into lying about my mother during the custody battle, the subsequent estrangement from her and my siblings, the inappropriate relationship with Rita and the secrecy surrounding it—have resulted in longer periods of depression and their resistance to all treatments but the most radical, which is ECT. This is because the ECT, with its accompanying memory loss, allows me to dissociate from the present triggering event that reminds me of past traumas.

Studies have shown that these types of severe events during childhood often cause the adult bipolar patient to take three times longer to recover from depression despite medication and therapy. Perhaps even more troubling is another study that found such events are more likely to cause episodes after *any* new life events, even those that are not in and of themselves traumatic. It is no coincidence that each time I land a job, often at Fortune 500 companies, a period of mania or depression is not far behind. This has rendered me incapable of holding down all but the simplest jobs and only for very brief periods.

My guilt, justified or not, over abandoning my mother or betraying my father with Rita is often too much for me to bear. Mania is my only escape from this reality, which is why, in addition to the fear of the inevitable depression to follow, I never want the high to end. The mania also gives me the only sense of control, however false, that I've ever had over my own life. When I am manic, there is nothing I cannot have or do. There is no one I cannot not be, whether it's a doctor or starting quarterback for the Jets.

I believe—and Kevin agrees—that my near-psychotic obsession with professional sports stems from a desire to reestablish a relationship with my father. We had always bonded over sports both individually with my father and as a family when we travelled to watch my half brother's basketball games. Somewhere in my mind, I believe that if I were a professional athlete all would be forgiven. There would be no way my father could ignore me if I were a starring athlete. At last I would return to my place as the apple of his eye. The ultimate fantasy, of course, is to reunite the DeBlasi and Paladino families as they cheer me on at the Super Bowl or World Series.

That dream, however, would never be. Our beloved Grandma Jennie passed away just shy of her ninety-third birthday. As we all gathered for her funeral, one person was conspicuously absent: her Joseph, who she had idolized most of her life only to be cast aside by him for taking in her sick grandson. Dad's brother Mike was there, though. He had taken care of our grandmother ever since Dad disowned her. Uncle Mike barely acknowledged us at the funeral; the closeness we had shared with him as children had been replaced by his bitterness of always playing second to our father. It seemed our ties with the DeBlasis had finally been severed for good.

These days I don't examine myself or the whys and wherefores of my disease: I have spent far too much of my life doing that. Instead I live day by day, hour by hour, trying to enjoy the simple pleasures—playing pick-up basketball, watching television, or, my favorite, eating a good steak. My family continues to be my source of support both emotionally and financially. They know if I start talking about career plans, it is a sure indication that I am cycling up, and they intervene as best they can. If I am more withdrawn than usual, they keep a constant eye on me and pray the depression won't be too severe or last too long.

I may have been born to a lousy father, but God blessed me with two younger brothers who would walk through fire for me, not to mention a mother who never gave up on me, a stepfather who took me in no questions asked, and a wife who stuck by me after seeing me at my worst. We only hope that we can be a source of comfort to those suffering from bipolar and do not have this support. That's why I have written this book and why my mother joined NAMI (National Alliance on Mental Illness) and for several years held the position of president of the Melbourne chapter.

As is often the case in life, the profoundest truth is the simplest. After decades of hospitalizations and arrests, meds and shock treatment, of battling my past, my father, and my disease, it has all come down to the statement Grandma Jennie and Grandpa Frank made back in 1991: "The three brothers have to stick together."

Made in the USA
Middletown, DE
05 May 2021

39036025R00163